# POSH PANCAKES & Fancy Fritters

by Helen V. Fisher

# FISHER BOOKS

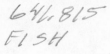

Publishers:

Bill Fisher
Helen Fisher
Howard Fisher
J. McCrary

Editor: Veronica Durie

Cover & Illustrations: David Fischer

Book Production: Paula Peterson

Published by Fisher Books
P. O. Box 38040
Tucson, Arizona 85740-8040
602-292-9080

Copyright © 1993 Fisher Books

Printed in U.S.A.
Printing 10 9 8 7 6 5 4 3 2

**Library of Congress
Cataloging-in-Publication Data**

Fisher, Helen V.
    Posh pancakes & fancy fritters / by Helen V. Fisher.
        p.    cm.
    Includes index.
    ISBN 1-55561-052-8 : $9.95
    1. Pancakes, waffles, etc.  I. Title.   II. Title: Posh pancakes and fancy fritters.
TX77.P34F57    1993
641.8'15—dc20                          93-7312
                                       CIP

Notice: The information in this book is true and complete to the best of our knowledge. It is offered with no guarantees on the part of the author or Fisher Books. Author and publisher disclaim all liability in connection with use of this book.

# CONTENTS

▼

# Introduction

❧

Pancakes are found throughout the world in one form or another. They are eaten for breakfast, brunch, supper and desserts. France has the delicate *crêpe;* in Hungary this same delicacy is called *palacsinta;* Germany knows it as *palatschinken.* Generally they're served as dessert, but they are also wrapped around nonsweet or savory fillings. Italy boasts of its *frittata,* usually filled with a variety of vegetables and Spain claims a similar potato pancake and calls it *tortilla.* This is not to be confused with the flat flour or cornmeal Mexican tortilla, a staple used in a myriad of ways. And of course the Chinese have *Mandarin* pancakes.

The United States has a variety of regional names including *pancakes, hot cakes, flapjacks* and *flannel cakes.* These tasty, easy-to-prepare cakes were always welcome at the big, satisfying breakfasts or light suppers our hard-working farm ancestors thrived on.

Pancakes are quickly made from flour or grain, liquid and seasonings that are mixed together and cooked on a griddle. Usually, leavening, eggs and oil are added.

*Fritter,* which probably comes from the Old French or Vulgar Latin words meaning *to fry,* usually refers to a cake-like patty that is either sautéed or deep-fried. Generally, fritters will contain cooked meats, fish or vegetables in a light batter. But not to be overlooked are the delightful fruit fritters.

You don't need special equipment to make pancakes. Use a nonstick griddle, electric fry pan or your favorite skillet—all will do the job. For best results, preheat the griddle or skillet. If necessary, lightly oil the surface before you begin pouring the batter.

If you are not sure if the griddle temperature is correct, make one pancake as a sample. After bubbles appear and you turn the pancake over, the second side cooks in about half the time of the first. Adjust the heat as necessary at this point.

There are a few recipes for yeast pancakes in the book and they require slightly different treatment. For these pancakes it is best to keep the heat on medium because they need longer, slower cooking.

## Ingredients

*Flours:*

Various flours and grains are called for in these recipes. All-purpose flour is usually mixed with wheat, rye or cornmeal, because these flours used alone are too heavy to make a tender pancake.

If you wish to experiment, try changing the ratios somewhat, but bear in mind that doing this will also change the amount of liquid required. For instance, rye flour and cornmeal absorb much more liquid than an equal amount of all-purpose flour.

It's a little difficult to give exact measurements because of variables caused by humidity, or the brand of flour. The amounts called for work well for me in a rather dry climate. Feel free to add a little more liquid, a tablespoon at a time, to reach the pouring consistency you desire.

*Milk products:*

To offer options that might not have occurred to you, I

have used various dairy products. How many times have you been out of fresh milk and didn't know what else to use? You can substitute equal amounts of yogurt, cottage cheese, ricotta cheese, or even juices. Evaporated canned milk can be used undiluted for a richer flavor, or diluted in half with water. Both dry buttermilk or milk powders will need water added to equal the amount of fresh milk called for in the recipe.

*Leavening:*

Baking powder is the most commonly used leavening agent.

However, if an acid such as molasses, buttermilk, soured milk or orange juice is called for, baking soda is also required. A combination of cream of tartar and baking soda can be used if baking powder is not available. If yeast is used, additional leavening is not usually required.

*Eggs:*

All recipes were tested with large size eggs. Liquid egg substitutes can be successfully used in all recipes except the Ginger-Pear Puff, page 120.

## Quantity

The number of pancakes in a recipe depends entirely on you. I have used one-fourth cup of batter for each four- to five-inch pancake. The exception to this is in a few rich dessert pancakes where I have indicated a smaller amount. If you prefer smaller ones like the dollar size, use about a tablespoon of batter. The yield will be three to four times greater than that listed in the recipe.

A simple way to keep pancakes warm while making them is to cover the plate with a colander. Most of the heat remains, and the holes let the steam escape so the pancakes will not become soggy. Or place pancakes on a plate in a warm oven until serving.

## Storing and reheating

Pancakes can be wrapped in plastic wrap or foil and refrigerated or double wrapped and frozen. If you choose to freeze pancakes, I recommend putting three or four in each package. Placing a sheet of waxed paper or foil between them makes removal and separation much easier.

Unwrap the package, removing the waxed-paper or foil dividers, and reheat in a microwave oven on HIGH (100%) for about 1 minute until hot. Do not overheat, as this causes them to toughen. They can also be heated in the oven. Place pancakes on a cookie sheet and cover with foil. Heat at 325F (165C) for 12 to 15 minutes. These times are based on Buttermilk-Mix or Traditional Pancake-Mix pancakes. If your pancakes contain nuts or fruits, warming time must be slightly longer.

# TRADITIONAL PLUS, PANCAKES

*Posh Pancakes & Fancy Fritters* is divided into sweet and savory (nonsweet) categories. I have provided a topping or sauce for each pancake or fritter with suggestions for alternatives. This makes a more complete dish and hopefully will encourage you to consider pancakes and fritters as something more than a Sunday breakfast treat. They are wonderfully quick and uncomplicated to put together. Most ingredients are combined in one bowl and I have tried to make the toppings just as simple.

Shrove Tuesday, the day before Ash Wednesday, is the perfect occasion to look again at your traditional pancake recipes. This year you may want to browse through the savory nonsweet recipes and make pancakes your entrée. Or, why not go for an extravagant dessert like Mocha Hazelnut Pancakes, page 42, served with Mocha and Grand Marnier Sauces, page 43, Enjoy a last fling before Lent!

# Recipes

Buttermilk Pancake Mix

Buttermilk-Mix Pancakes & Variations

Traditional Pancake Mix

Traditional-Mix Pancakes & Variation

Whole-Wheat Pancakes
*Broiled Cinnamon Pineapple*

New England Buckwheat Cakes
*Stewed Apple Slices*

Yankee Rum-Raisin Pancakes
*Orange-Raisin Sauce*

Bacon Yeast Pancakes
*Cilantro Scramble*

Whole-Wheat & Raisin Yeast Cakes
*Spicy Dried Fruit*

Sourdough Starter

Sourdough Pancakes

Blue-Corn Cakes
*Lemony Walnut Sauce*

Ginger-Pear Puff & Variations

Banana Pancakes
*Honeyed Blackberries*

Sour-Cream Pancakes
*Tart Cherry Sauce*

# Buttermilk Pancake Mix

*I admit being very partial to this mix. The secret ingredient for making extra-tender pancakes is dry buttermilk powder. You'll find it in the baking section or canned and powdered-milk section at your market.*

**8 cups all-purpose flour**
**2 cups dry buttermilk powder**
**1-1/2 teaspoons salt**
**1/4 cup baking powder**
**2 tablespoons baking soda**
**1/2 cup sugar**

In a large bowl, stir all ingredients until thoroughly combined. If using a blender or food processor to combine ingredients, volume will be slightly increased. Store mix in an airtight container. Use within 3 months. Makes 8 recipes.

## Variation

*Whole-Wheat Buttermilk Mix:* Use 3 cups all-purpose flour and add 4 cups whole-wheat flour and 1 cup cracked wheat. Use remaining ingredients listed in mix.

**Tip:** After preparing a mix, store it in an airtight container and use within three months. The mix can be kept in the refrigerator or freezer. If you do this, measure out the amount you are using and let it come to room temperature before blending with other ingredients.

# Buttermilk-Mix Pancakes

*Now you can enjoy the convenience of having your own mix at your fingertips. Try any of these pancakes with one of the flavored butters in the More Relishes & Toppings chapter, page 110.*

**1-1/2 cups Buttermilk Pancake Mix, opposite**
**1 cup water**
**1 egg**
**2 tablespoons melted butter or oil**
**1 teaspoon vanilla extract**

Preheat a nonstick griddle or lightly oiled heavy skillet. Combine all ingredients in a medium bowl, blender or food processor; mix until blended.

Using preheated griddle or skillet, pour or spoon about 1/4 cup batter for each pancake. Cook pancakes until bubbles appear and edges look slightly dry. Turn over and continue cooking until lightly browned. Serve with syrup or your favorite topping.

Makes 10 to 12 pancakes.

## Variations

*Southwestern Buttermilk Pancakes:* Use 1 cup Buttermilk Pancake Mix, 1/4 cup cornmeal and 1/4 cup buckwheat flour with remaining ingredients listed in recipe.

*Spicy Buttermilk Pancakes:* Add 1/2 teaspoon ground cinnamon, 1/4 teaspoon ground nutmeg, 1/4 teaspoon ground allspice and 1 teaspoon dried or grated fresh orange peel to remaining ingredients listed in recipe.

*Raisin-Nut Buttermilk Pancakes:* Add 1/2 cup raisins, 1/4 cup chopped nuts and 1/4 cup bran flakes to remaining ingredients listed in recipe.

# Traditional Pancake Mix

*You can make your own mix in less time than it takes to go to the store. If you have a dietary limitation such as no salt, you can eliminate that ingredient and still have a great-tasting pancake.*

**8 cups all-purpose flour**
**2 cups dry milk powder**
**1/2 cup baking powder**
**1 tablespoon salt**
**1/2 cup sugar**
**1 cup butter-flavored shortening**

In a large bowl, stir dry ingredients together. Cut in shortening with a pastry blender. If using a blender or food processor, blend together in 4 batches. Store mix in an airtight container. Use within 3 months. Makes 8 recipes.

## Variation

*Oatmeal Pancake Mix:* Use 3 cups all-purpose flour and add 4 cups oatmeal and 1 cup oat bran. Use remaining ingredients listed in mix.

# *Traditional-Mix Pancakes*

*With your dry ingredients all mixed, you can have your batter ready in a minute.*

**1-1/2 cups Traditional Pancake Mix, opposite**
**1 cup water**
**1 egg**
**1 teaspoon vanilla extract**

Preheat a nonstick griddle or lightly oiled heavy skillet. Combine all ingredients in a medium bowl, blender or food processor; mix until blended.

Using preheated griddle or skillet, pour or spoon about 1/4 cup batter for each pancake. Cook pancakes until bubbles appear and edges look slightly dry. Turn over and continue cooking until lightly browned. Serve with butter, syrup or fruit. Makes 10 to 12 pancakes.

## Variations

*Apple-Walnut Pancakes:* Add 1 chopped small apple and 1/3 cup chopped walnuts to remaining ingredients listed in recipe.

*Almond-Cherry Pancakes:* Add 3 tablespoons chopped almonds and 2/3 cup chopped dried or fresh cherries to remaining ingredients listed in recipe.

*Banana-Coconut Pancakes:* Add 1 chopped banana and 1/2 cup flaked coconut to remaining ingredients listed in recipe.

*Pineapple-Date Pancakes:* Add 1/2 cup drained canned pineapple and 1/4 cup chopped dates to remaining ingredients listed in recipe.

# Whole-Wheat Pancakes

*For a crunchy texture, add two teaspoons of toasted sesame seeds, or chopped nuts. These flavors combine ideally with whole-wheat.*

**1 cup milk**
**1 egg**
**1/2 cup all-purpose flour**
**1/2 cup whole-wheat flour**
**1/4 cup wheat germ**
**2 teaspoons baking powder**
**1 teaspoon baking soda**
**2 tablespoons melted butter or oil**
**1 tablespoon molasses**
**1 tablespoon brown sugar**

Preheat a nonstick griddle or lightly oiled heavy skillet. Combine all ingredients in a medium bowl, blender or food processor; mix until blended.

Using preheated griddle or skillet, pour or spoon about 1/4 cup batter for each pancake. Cook pancakes until bubbles appear and edges look slightly dry. Turn over and continue cooking until lightly browned. Serve with Broiled Cinnamon Pineapple, opposite, or Orange-Raisin Sauce, page 11. Makes 10 to 12 pancakes.

# *Broiled Cinnamon Pineapple*

*The core of a small pineapple is usually quite tender, so only remove it if it appears to be fibrous.*

**1 small fresh pineapple, peeled, cut into 1/2-inch slices or 1 (16-oz.) can pineapple slices, drained**
**2 to 3 tablespoons melted butter or margarine**
**1/4 cup firmly packed brown sugar**
**1/2 teaspoon ground cinnamon**

Place pineapple slices on a broiler pan. Cut each slice into fourths. Brush with butter or margarine. In a cup, combine sugar and cinnamon. Sprinkle over pineapple. Broil until bubbling. Do not turn pieces over. Serve at once.

## Variation

Omit pineapple and substitute apricot or plum halves. Use remaining ingredients listed in recipe.

# New England Buckwheat Cakes

*What better way to start the day! These are wonderful topped with real maple syrup and Stewed Apple Slices.*

**1 cup all-purpose flour**
**1/2 cup buckwheat flour**
**2 tablespoons sugar**
**2-1/2 teaspoons baking powder**
**1 egg**
**3 tablespoons melted butter, margarine or oil**
**1-1/2 cups water**
**1/3 cup dry milk powder**
**1 teaspoon vanilla extract or maple flavoring**

**Maple syrup**

Preheat a nonstick griddle or lightly oiled heavy skillet. Combine all ingredients in a medium bowl, blender or food processor; mix until blended.

Using preheated griddle or skillet, pour or spoon about 1/4 cup batter for each pancake. Cook pancakes until bubbles appear and edges look slightly dry. Turn over and continue cooking until lightly browned. Serve with maple syrup, Stewed Apple Slices, opposite, or Orange-Honey Butter, page 114. Makes 10 to 12 pancakes.

# *Stewed Apple Slices*

*Choose firm cooking apples like pippins or Granny Smiths because they retain their shape better than the softer varieties such as Gravenstein.*

**2 medium apples, peeled, cored, sliced**
**3/4 cup apple cider or apple juice**
**1/3 cup maple syrup or honey**
**1 cinnamon stick**
**3 whole cloves**

In a small saucepan, combine all ingredients and bring to a boil. Reduce heat and simmer until apples are tender. Remove cinnamon stick and cloves. Serve warm. Apples can be refrigerated in a covered container up to 2 weeks.

## Variation

Substitute apricot halves or peach slices for apples. Use remaining ingredients listed in recipe.

# Yankee Rum-Raisin Pancakes

*Early New England settlers grew rye and were fond of using it in many ways. Rum was always present so it was a natural combination. In those days they made a mixture of sugar and vinegar and spread it on their pancakes. I much prefer maple syrup.*

**1 cup rye flour**
**1/2 cup all-purpose flour**
**1 egg**
**1-1/2 cups milk**
**2 tablespoons sugar**
**2 tablespoons molasses**
**1/2 teaspoon cream of tartar**
**1/2 teaspoon baking powder**
**1/4 cup rum or apple juice or 1 tablespoon rum**
**extract plus 3 tablespoons milk**
**3 tablespoons chopped raisins or dried currants**
**2 tablespoons oil**

Preheat a nonstick griddle or lightly oiled heavy skillet. Combine all ingredients in a medium bowl, blender or food processor; mix until blended.

Using preheated griddle or skillet, pour or spoon about 1/4 cup batter for each pancake. Cook pancakes until bubbles appear and edges look slightly dry. Turn over and continue cooking until lightly browned. Serve with Orange-Raisin Sauce, opposite, or Stewed Apple Slices, page 9. Makes 15 to 16 pancakes.

# Orange-Raisin Sauce

*Although raisin sauce isn't seasonal, I prefer to serve this during cold-weather months. Enjoy plump raisins in an orange sauce.*

**1/4 cup water**
**3 tablespoons sugar**
**1 tablespoon cornstarch**
**3/4 cup orange juice**
**1/2 cup raisins**
**1 tablespoon rum extract**
**1 tablespoon butter or margarine**

In a small saucepan, combine water, sugar, cornstarch and orange juice; stir until cornstarch is dissolved. Add raisins and cook over medium heat, stirring, until mixture thickens. Remove from heat and add rum extract. Stir in butter or margarine until melted. Serve warm. Makes about 1-1/2 cups.

# Bacon Yeast Pancakes

*The yeast lends a slightly different flavor as well as texture.*

**1 (1/4-oz.) pkg. active dry yeast (1 tablespoon)**
**1 tablespoon sugar**
**1/4 cup warm water**
**2 eggs**
**1-1/4 cups all-purpose flour**
**1 cup milk**
**2 tablespoons oil**
**3 bacon strips, cooked, crumbled**

In a cup, dissolve yeast and sugar in warm water. Combine all ingredients in a medium bowl, blender or food processor; blend briefly. Let stand about 20 minutes before cooking. Batter will be thin.

Preheat a nonstick griddle or lightly oiled heavy skillet. Using preheated griddle or skillet, pour or spoon about 1/4 cup batter for each pancake. Cook pancakes over medium heat until bubbles appear and edges look slightly dry. Turn over and continue cooking until lightly browned. Serve with Cilantro Scramble, opposite, or a fruit syrup. Makes 10 to 12 pancakes.

## Variation

Omit bacon and substitute 1/3 cup chopped cooked ham. Use remaining ingredients listed in recipe.

# *Cilantro Scramble*

*Enliven ordinary eggs with western flavors. Serve on the side or on top of a small pancake stack.*

**2 tablespoons butter or margarine**
**2 green onions, chopped**
**2 tablespoons chopped fresh cilantro**
**1/4 teaspoon dried-leaf oregano**
**4 eggs**
**Chili powder to taste**

In a medium skillet, melt butter or margarine. Add onions, cilantro and oregano; sauté briefly. Add eggs all at once and using a fork, stir and turn mixture quickly until cooked as desired. Sprinkle with chili powder to taste. Serve at once. Makes 4 servings.

# Whole-Wheat & Raisin Yeast Cakes

*When you are cooking for a family gathering this larger recipe is just what you need. Wheat germ and raisins add sweetness and texture.*

**1 (1/4-oz.) pkg. active dry yeast (1 tablespoon)**
**2 teaspoons sugar**
**1/2 cup warm water or milk**
**1 cup water**
**1 cup milk**
**1 egg**
**1 tablespoon molasses or honey**
**3 tablespoons melted butter or oil**
**1-3/4 cups whole-wheat flour**
**1/4 cup wheat germ**
**1 cup all-purpose flour**
**1 teaspoon baking soda**
**1/2 cup raisins**

**Canadian bacon**

In a cup, dissolve yeast and 1/2 cup sugar in warm water or milk. Combine all ingredients in a large bowl, blender or food processor; blend briefly. Let stand about 30 minutes before cooking. Batter will be thin.

Preheat a nonstick griddle or lightly oiled heavy skillet. Using preheated griddle or skillet, pour or spoon about 1/4 cup batter for each pancake. Cook pancakes over medium heat until bubbles appear and edges look slightly dry. Turn over and continue cooking until lightly browned. Serve with broiled Canadian bacon and Spicy Dried Fruit, opposite, or Maple-Pecan Butter, page 114. Makes about 36 pancakes.

# *Spicy Dried Fruit*

*Sturdy whole-wheat pancakes beg for a topping full of natural sweetness.*

**2 cups dried fruits, prunes, apples, apricots,
  peaches or pears**
**1-1/2 cups water**
**1 cup apple juice**
**1 cinnamon stick**
**1/4 teaspoon whole allspice**
**1/4 teaspoon whole cloves**
**1/4 teaspoon ground nutmeg**
**1/4 cup firmly packed brown sugar**
**1 tablespoon grated orange peel**
**1/4 cup orange juice**

**Vanilla yogurt**

In a large saucepan, combine dried fruits, water, apple juice, cinnamon, allspice, cloves, nutmeg and sugar. Bring to a boil; reduce heat and simmer until fruits are plumped and tender. Stir in orange peel and juice. This may be made ahead as the flavor improves on standing. Refrigerate in a covered container until needed. Serve warm with a dollop of vanilla yogurt.

# Sourdough Starter

*Sourdough starter should never be stored in a metal bowl or container. A glass or ceramic container is best. Prepared sourdough starters are also available; follow package directions.*

**1 (1/4-oz.) pkg. active dry yeast (1 tablespoon)**
**2 cups warm water**
**2 cups all-purpose flour**

In a large bowl or glass or plastic pitcher, combine yeast and warm water. Let stand 5 to 10 minutes. Slowly stir in flour. Cover and set in a draft-free area. Let stand overnight or at least 6 to 12 hours. A stronger flavor develops if starter ferments at room temperature 2 to 3 days. It will be bubbly. Stir it well before using. Remove starter needed for recipe.

To replenish starter, beat in equal amounts of warm water and flour. Cover and let stand at room temperature overnight. Cover container, allowing room for expansion, refrigerate. Mixture will separate; stir and mix in liquid before using. Replenish every 7 to 10 days.

## Variation
*Whole-Wheat Sourdough Starter:* For flour use 1-1/2 cups whole-wheat flour and 1/2 cup all-purpose flour. Use with remaining ingredients listed in recipe.

# Sourdough Pancakes

*Using the starter gives these pancakes a unique flavor and pleasantly chewy texture.*

**1 egg
1 cup milk
1 tablespoon honey or sugar
3 tablespoons oil
1 cup sourdough starter of choice, opposite
1 teaspoon baking powder
1/2 teaspoon baking soda
1-1/4 cups all-purpose flour**

In a large bowl, beat together egg, milk, honey or sugar and oil. Stir in starter, baking powder, baking soda and flour. Stir until ingredients are combined, do not beat.

Preheat a nonstick griddle or lightly oiled heavy skillet. Using preheated griddle or skillet, pour or spoon about 1/4 cup batter for each pancake. Cook pancakes over medium heat until bubbles break and edges look slightly dry. Turn over and continue cooking until lightly browned. Sourdough pancakes require a little longer cooking. Serve with honey, syrup or powdered sugar. Makes 20 to 24 pancakes.

**Variations**

*Sourdough Apple Pancakes:* Add 3/4 cup chopped peeled apple, 1/4 teaspoon ground cinnamon and 1/4 teaspoon grated nutmeg to remaining ingredients listed in recipe.

*Sourdough Raisin-Walnut Pancakes:* Omit milk and replace with 1 cup apple juice. Add 1/2 cup raisins, 1/2 cup chopped walnuts and 1 teaspoon vanilla extract to remaining ingredients listed in recipe.

# *Blue-Corn Cakes*

*Blue corn has a distinctive nut-like taste. Here it's enhanced by pairing it with toasted walnuts. You can use raw nuts, but I feel toasting brings out more flavor.*

**3/4 cup blue corn meal**
**3/4 cup all-purpose flour**
**4 teaspoons baking powder**
**2 teaspoons baking soda**
**2 tablespoons sugar**
**1 egg**
**1-1/2 cups soured milk**
**2 tablespoons oil**
**1/4 cup toasted chopped walnuts**

Preheat a nonstick griddle or lightly oiled heavy skillet. Combine all ingredients except walnuts, in a medium bowl, blender or food processor; blend briefly. Stir in walnuts.

Using preheated griddle or skillet, pour or spoon about 1/4 cup batter for each pancake. Cook pancakes until bubbles appear and edges look slightly dry. Turn over and continue cooking until lightly browned. Serve with Lemony Walnut Sauce, opposite, or Honeyed Blackberries, page 23. Makes 10 to 12 pancakes.

**Tip:** To make soured milk, add 1-1/2 tablespoons lemon juice or white vinegar to 1-1/2 cups sweet milk; stir and let stand 5 minutes.

# *Lemony Walnut Sauce*

*Crunchy chopped nuts are teamed up with tangy lemon.*

**1/3 cup thawed frozen lemonade concentrate**
**1 cup water**
**2 tablespoons cornstarch**
**2 teaspoons grated lemon peel**
**1 tablespoon butter or margarine**
**1/3 cup toasted chopped walnuts**

In a small saucepan, stir together lemonade concentrate, water, cornstarch and lemon peel. Cook, stirring over medium heat until thickened. Remove from heat; stir in butter or margarine and walnuts. Serve warm. Makes about 1 cup.

# Ginger-Pear Puff

*Firm, ripe Bartlett pears are my favorite for this special dish. If you use the firmer Bosc or Anjou pears, I recommend cutting them into ten or twelve slices.*

**3 tablespoons butter or margarine**
**1 or 2 firm, ripe Bartlett pears**
**4 eggs**
**2/3 cup all-purpose flour**
**2/3 cup milk**
**3 tablespoons granulated sugar**
**1/4 cup orange juice**
**4 teaspoons chopped crystallized ginger**
**2 tablespoons brown sugar**

Preheat oven to 425F (220C). Melt butter or margarine in a 9-inch deep-dish pie pan or quiche pan. Peel and seed pears; cut lengthwise into eighths. Place pear slices in melted butter or margarine, turning to coat all sides. Arrange slices in a pinwheel design.

In a medium bowl, blender or food processor, combine eggs, flour, milk, granulated sugar, orange juice and 1 teaspoon chopped ginger; blend thoroughly. Carefully pour into center of pan with pear slices. In a cup, combine remaining 3 teaspoons chopped ginger and brown sugar. Sprinkle over batter.

Bake in preheated oven 20 to 25 minutes until golden brown and puffed. Most of the puffing takes place in the last 5 to 7 minutes. Serve at once. Makes 4 to 6 servings.

## Puff Variations

The Dutch call their oven-baked pancakes *pannekoek*. Perhaps pears are not your favorite fruit or they are not always available. Here are some alternatives:

*Almond-Nectarine Puff:* Omit pears and ginger and replace with 2 or 3 sliced, peeled nectarines and 1/2 teaspoon almond extract. Use remaining ingredients and follow recipe directions.

*Cinnamon-Apple Puff:* Omit pears and replace with 2 large sliced, peeled apples. Omit ginger and combine 1/4 teaspoon ground cinnamon with brown sugar in recipe. Use remaining ingredients and follow recipe directions.

*Orange-Pecan Puff:* Omit pears and add 1 tablespoon orange liqueur or 1 teaspoon orange extract. Omit ginger and combine 2 tablespoons toasted chopped pecans with brown sugar in recipe. Use remaining ingredients and follow recipe directions.

**Tip:** If you have any fruit puff left over, cover with foil or plastic wrap and refrigerate. To reheat, cover with foil and bake at 425F (220C) until hot. Or cover with plastic wrap and microwave at MEDIUM (50%) power until heated. The pancake will repuff slightly, but not reach its original height.

# *Banana Pancakes*

*Sweet bananas in the pancakes are enhanced by a topping of honey-spiced blackberries. In Italy, it is common to accent fresh berries with a dash of pepper. It really tastes great.*

**1-1/2 cups all-purpose flour**
**1 tablespoon baking powder**
**1 cup water**
**3/4 cup sweetened condensed milk**
**2 tablespoons oil**
**2 medium bananas, sliced**
**1/2 teaspoon banana flavoring or vanilla extract**
**2 egg whites**

Preheat a nonstick griddle or lightly oiled heavy skillet. In a blender, food processor or medium bowl, combine flour, baking powder, water, sweetened condensed milk and oil until blended. Stir in sliced bananas and banana flavoring or vanilla. In a small bowl, beat egg whites until stiff; fold into batter.

Using preheated griddle or skillet, pour or spoon about 1/4 cup batter for each pancake. Cook pancakes until bubbles appear and edges look slightly dry. Turn over and continue cooking until lightly browned. Serve topped with Honeyed Blackberries, opposite, or Jamberry Butter, page 115. Makes 18 to 20 pancakes.

# *Honeyed Blackberries*

*Succulent berries with just a touch of spice.*

**1/4 cup honey**
**1 tablespoon orange juice**
**Grated nutmeg**
**Ground black pepper, optional**
**4 cups fresh or 1 (16-oz.) pkg. drained**
  **thawed, frozen blackberries**

In a cup, blend honey with orange juice. If honey is stiff, warm it slightly before adding juice. Add a dash of nutmeg and black pepper, if desired; stir to blend. Taste and add more nutmeg and black pepper, if desired. Drizzle honey mixture over blackberries and lightly toss to coat. Makes 4 cups.

## Variation

Omit honey and black pepper. Substitute raspberries or strawberries and sweeten to taste with sugar.

# *Sour-Cream Pancakes*

*Our illustrator, David Fischer, shares his
grandmother's special family recipe.*

**3/4 cup dairy sour cream**
**1/3 cup small-curd cottage cheese**
**2 eggs**
**1/2 cup all-purpose flour**
**1/2 teaspoon baking soda**
**1/2 teaspoon salt**

Preheat a nonstick griddle or lightly oiled heavy skillet.
Combine all ingredients in a medium bowl, blender or
food processor; mix until blended.

Using preheated griddle or skillet, pour or spoon about
1/4 cup batter for each pancake. Cook pancakes until
bubbles appear and edges look slightly dry. Turn over
and continue cooking until lightly browned. Serve with
Tart Cherry Sauce, opposite, fresh berries or strawberry
preserves. Makes 9 to 10 pancakes.

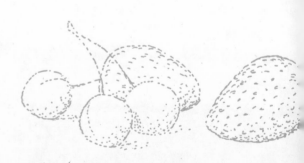

# *Tart Cherry Sauce*

*Blueberries or gooseberries can be substituted for the cherries.*

**1/2 teaspoon almond extract**
**1/2 cup plain yogurt**
**1/2 cup sweetened whipped topping or whipped cream**
**1 (16-oz.) can pitted tart cherries**

In a medium bowl, stir together almond extract, yogurt and whipped topping or whipped cream. Drain cherries, reserving 2 tablepoons juice. Fold cherries and reserved juice into yogurt mixture. Makes about 3 cups.

## Variation

For a more festive presentation, double the amount of sauce and layer it between pancakes using 3 or 4 in each stack.

# PANCAKES WITH FLAIR

Recipes in this chapter are especially good for a leisurely weekend breakfast or a brunch for friends. During the winter months, a large electric grill or skillet can be used indoors for buffet serving. When the mornings become warmer, move your brunch to porch or patio. Make up the toppings the day before and the batters an hour or two ahead. Set pitchers of juice on the table along with several platters of attractively cut fresh fruit.

Many of the nonsweet savory pancakes and fritters make ideal brunch fare. The Bacon Yeast Pancakes, page 12, would be an excellent choice especially if some chopped smoked salmon is stirred into the accompanying Cilantro Scramble, page 13. If you are looking for something more substantial to satisfy mid-morning appetites, consider the Italian Sausage & Corn Cakes, page 80. Provide a choice of toppings and relishes so guests can create their own combinations. I can guarantee that no one will leave your brunch hungry!

# Recipes

### Lemon-Poppy-Seed Pancakes
*Lemon-Whip Topping with Blackberries*

### Ricotta & Fruit Pancakes
*Citrus Sauce*

### Cinnamon-Walnut Crumb Cakes
*Raspberry Sauce*

### Sweet-Potato Pancakes
*Papaya Relish*

### Elegant Raspberries-&-Cream Pancakes
*Orange Cream*

### Deluxe Cottage-Cheese Pancakes
*Broiled Peaches*

### Apple Fritters
*Blackberry Sauce*

### Mocha-Hazelnut Pancakes
*Chocolate Mocha Sauce*
*Grand Marnier Sauce*

### Double-Chocolate Oatmeal Pancakes
*Brandy-Chocolate Sauce*

### Apricot-Chiffon Pancakes
*Nutmeg Meringue*

# *Lemon-Poppy-Seed Pancakes*

*Blueberries served with these lemon pancakes creates a delicious combination. Poppy seeds add just the right amount of crunchy texture.*

**1 cup lemon-flavored yogurt**
**1/4 cup water**
**1 teaspoon grated lemon peel**
**1 tablespoon lemon juice**
**1 cup all-purpose flour**
**1 teaspoon baking soda**
**1 tablespoon sugar**
**1-1/2 tablespoons poppy seeds**

Preheat a nonstick griddle or lightly oiled heavy skillet. Combine all ingredients in a medium bowl, blender or food processor; mix until blended.

Using preheated griddle or skillet, pour or spoon about 1/4 cup batter for each pancake. Cook pancakes until bubbles appear and edges look slightly dry. Turn over and continue cooking until lightly browned. Serve with Lemon-Whip Topping with Blueberries, opposite. Makes 10 to 12 pancakes.

## Variation

*Strawberry Pancakes:* Omit poppy seeds. Substitute strawberry-flavored yogurt for lemon-flavored yogurt in pancakes and topping, opposite. Substitute 1 cup sliced strawberries for blueberries in topping. Use remaining ingredients listed in recipes.

# *Lemon-Whip Topping with Blueberries*

*A tangy flavored yogurt is lightened with whipped cream.*

**1/2 cup whipping cream or sweetened
  whipped topping**
**1 cup lemon-flavored yogurt**
**1 teaspoon grated lemon peel**
**1 cup fresh or thawed frozen blueberries**

Whip whipping cream. In a small serving bowl, fold together whipped cream or topping, yogurt and lemon peel. Serve over pancakes; sprinkle with blueberries. Makes about 2 cups.

## Variation

Omit lemon-flavored yogurt and substitute another flavored yogurt. Top with berries or fresh fruit of your choice.

# Ricotta & Fruit Pancakes

*Reminiscent of tutti frutti, sweet glazed fruits accent the light cheese flavor. Citrus Sauce adds color and a hint of tartness.*

**1/2 cup all-purpose flour**
**1 tablespoon sugar**
**2 teaspoons baking powder**
**2 eggs**
**1-1/4 cups ricotta cheese**
**1/4 cup milk**
**1/2 teaspoon lemon extract**
**1/2 cup glazed mixed fruits such as cherries, citron, orange, pineapple**

Preheat a nonstick griddle or lightly oiled heavy skillet. Combine all ingredients except mixed fruits in a blender or food processor; mix until blended. Stir in fruits and pulse to chop fruits slightly.

Using preheated griddle or skillet, pour or spoon about 1/4 cup batter for each pancake. Cook pancakes until bubbles appear and edges look slightly dry. Turn over and continue cooking until lightly browned. Serve with Citrus Sauce, opposite, or Raspberry Sauce, page 33. Makes 10 to 12 pancakes.

# *Citrus Sauce*

*Not overly sweet, this combination of orange and lemon juices provides a delightful contrast to the glazed fruits.*

**2 tablespoons cornstarch**
**1/4 cup sugar**
**1-1/4 cups orange juice**
**1 tablespoon grated orange peel**
**2 tablespoons lemon juice**
**1 tablespoon butter**
**1 tablespoon rum, if desired**

In a small saucepan, stir together cornstarch, sugar, orange juice, orange peel and lemon juice. Cook, stirring constantly, until thickened and mixture is clear. Remove from heat and add butter and rum, if desired. Stir until butter is melted. Serve warm or chilled. Makes about 1-3/4 cups.

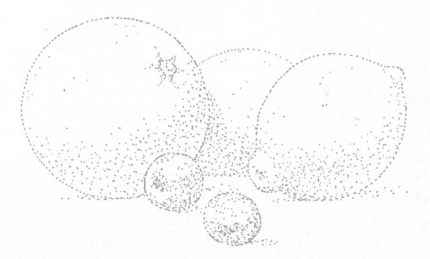

# Cinnamon-Walnut Crumb Cakes

*An unusually tender pancake that is equally good
served at room temperature for dessert.*

**3 to 4 bread slices**
**1 cup evaporated milk**
**1/2 cup water**
**2 egg whites**
**2 tablespoons brown sugar**
**1-1/2 teaspoons ground cinnamon**
**3/4 cup all-purpose flour**
**1 tablespoon baking powder**
**3 tablespoons melted butter, margarine or oil**
**1/2 cup chopped walnuts**

In a blender or food processor, process enough bread to
make 2 cups fine crumbs. Place in a medium bowl and
set aside. Combine milk and water; pour over crumbs.
Stir to combine thoroughly; let stand 10 minutes. Preheat
a nonstick griddle or lightly oiled heavy skillet.

In a medium bowl, whip egg whites until stiff; set aside.
Stir sugar, cinnamon, flour, baking powder, melted
butter, margarine or oil and walnuts into crumb mixture;
mix together until blended. Fold in whipped egg whites.

Using preheated griddle or skillet, pour or spoon about
1/4 cup batter for each pancake. Cook pancakes until
bubbles appear and edges look slightly dry. Turn over
and continue cooking until lightly browned. Serve with
Raspberry Sauce, opposite, or Orange Cream, page 37.
Makes 10 to 12 pancakes.

**Tip:** To make crumb cakes ahead, place them on a
cookie sheet as you make them and cover with a cloth
towel to keep them from drying out.

# *Raspberry Sauce*

*This pretty sauce accents almost any sweet pancake.*
*Use it often and discover new flavor combinations.*

**2 cups fresh or 1 (12- or 16-oz.) pkg. thawed, frozen,**
**unsweetened raspberries**
**Water**
**1/3 to 1/2 cup sugar**
**1 tablespoon cornstarch**
**1/4 teaspoon ground cinnamon**
**2 teaspoons lemon or orange juice**
**2 teaspoons butter or margarine**

Drain thawed frozen raspberries, reserving juice. Add water to reserved juice to make 1 cup. If using fresh raspberries, it will be necessary to add 1 cup water or raspberry juice. Crush raspberries or pulse in a food processor. Press through a strainer to remove seeds. Discard seeds and place raspberry pulp in a small saucepan.

Add to reserved juice and water, sugar, cornstarch, cinnamon and raspberry pulp. Stirring constantly, cook over medium heat until thickened and clear. Remove from heat and stir in lemon or orange juice and butter or margarine. Makes about 2-3/4 cups.

# *Sweet-Potato Pancakes*

*Rich in vitamins, sweet potatoes are good for us as well as good tasting. Here's another way to serve them.*

**2/3 cup mashed, cooked, sweet potatoes**
**1 tablespoon sugar**
**1 tablespoon baking powder**
**3/4 cup milk**
**2 tablespoons melted butter or oil**
**2 egg whites**
**1/4 teaspoon ground cinnamon**
**1/4 teaspoon ground mace**
**1/4 cup flaked coconut, if desired**

Preheat a nonstick griddle or lightly oiled heavy skillet. Combine all ingredients except coconut, in a medium bowl, blender or food processor; mix until blended. Fold in coconut, if desired.

Using preheated griddle or skillet, pour or spoon about 1/4 cup batter for each pancake. Cook pancakes until bubbles appear and edges look slightly dry. Turn over and continue cooking until lightly browned. Serve with Papaya Relish, opposite, or Maple-Pecan Butter, page 114. Makes 12 to 15 pancakes.

**Variation**

Substitute pumpkin for sweet potatoes. If you cook your own fresh pumpkin, drain it well before using in any recipe.

# *Papaya Relish*

*Experience the wonderful flavors of the Hawaiian Islands.*

**1 ripe papaya**
**3 tablespoons lime or lemon juice**
**1/4 cup apricot jam**
**2 tablespoons dried currants or raisins**
**1/3 cup chopped macadamia nuts**
**1/4 cup shredded coconut**

Peel papaya; cut in half and remove seeds. If desired, reserve seeds for a papaya dressing. Chop papaya and place in a medium bowl. Sprinkle with 1 tablespoon lime or lemon juice. In a small bowl, stir remaining juice together with jam; add remaining ingredients. Pour over chopped papaya and gently toss. Cover and refrigerate until needed. Makes about 2-3/4 cups.

# Elegant Raspberries-&-Cream Pancakes

*For that memorable brunch, treat your guests to these picture-pretty, incredibly tender pancakes. Serve with both sauces for the ultimate indulgence.*

**1-1/2 cups all-purpose flour**
**2-1/2 teaspoons baking powder**
**3 tablespoons sugar**
**3 eggs**
**1-2/3 cups whipping cream**
**1/4 teaspoon almond extract**
**1/2 cup fresh raspberries or thawed frozen**
  **raspberries, drained**

Preheat a nonstick griddle or lightly oiled heavy skillet. In a medium bowl, blender or food processor, mix all ingredients except raspberries. If using a blender or processor, add raspberries and pulse briefly to chop berries. Or slightly crush raspberries and fold into batter.

Using preheated griddle or skillet, pour or spoon about 1/4 cup batter for each pancake. Cook pancakes until bubbles appear and edges look slightly dry. Turn over and continue cooking until lightly browned. Serve with Orange Cream, opposite, and Brandy-Chocolate Sauce, page 45. Makes 18 to 20.

# *Orange Cream*

*The addition of orange juice and peel lends both subtle color and taste appeal. For added variety, try substituting lime or lemon for the orange.*

**1 cup whipping cream**
**3 tablespoons powdered sugar**
**1 tablespoon orange juice**
**2 to 3 teaspoons grated orange peel**
**1-1/2 cups fresh raspberries or thawed frozen**
  **raspberries, drained**

In a small chilled bowl, combine whipping cream, sugar, orange juice and orange peel. Whip until cream mounds. Serve over pancakes and top with raspberries. Makes 1-1/2 to 2 cups.

# Deluxe Cottage-Cheese Pancakes

*Richer than most other recipes, this is also great with a sprinkle of lemon juice and powdered sugar.*

**6 eggs**
**1-1/2 cups small-curd cottage cheese**
**1 tablespoon sugar**
**1/2 teaspoon salt**
**1/2 cup all-purpose flour**
**1 teaspoon vanilla extract**

Preheat a nonstick griddle or lightly oiled heavy skillet. Combine all ingredients in a bowl, blender or food processor; mix until blended.

Using preheated griddle or skillet, pour or spoon about 1/4 cup batter for each pancake. Cook pancakes until bubbles appear and edges look slightly dry. Turn over and continue cooking until lightly browned. Serve with Broiled Peaches, opposite, or Raspberry Sauce, page 33. Makes 14 to 16 pancakes.

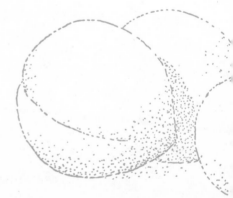

# Broiled Peaches

*Don't think broiling is for meat alone! Try any fresh firm fruit like pears, apples or pineapple.*

**4 fresh peaches, peeled, pitted, halved or halved**
 **canned peaches, drained**
**1 tablespoon lemon juice**
**Honey**
**Ground nutmeg or cinnamon**

Place peach halves cut-side up on a baking sheet. If using canned peaches, pat dry with paper towel. Drizzle lemon juice over peaches. Brush honey over entire cut surface of peaches. Sprinkle with dash of nutmeg or cinnamon. Broil on high until bubbling and lightly browned. Do not burn. Serve hot. Makes 8 peach halves.

# *Apple Fritters*

*My mother made apple fritters and we all loved them. Try other fruits or berries and you will rediscover an old favorite.*

**1-1/4 cups all-purpose flour**
**3 tablespoons sugar**
**1 teaspoon baking powder**
**1 cup milk or water**
**1 tablespoon oil**
**2 egg whites**
**3 apples, peeled, cored, sliced,**

**Oil for frying**

Combine flour, sugar, baking powder, milk or water and 1 tablespoon oil in a medium bowl, blender or food processor; mix until blended. Beat egg whites until stiff; fold into batter.

In a large skillet, heat 3 to 4 tablespoons oil. Carefully stir apple slices in batter. Spoon apple and batter into oil in batches. When edges begin to brown, turn and cook other side. Place on absorbent paper or paper towel. Serve at once or cover and keep warm in 325F (160C) oven. Makes 20 to 24.

Serve with Blackberry Sauce, opposite, or sprinkle with powdered sugar. Makes 4 servings.

# *Blackberry Sauce*

*I'm especially fond of the classic apple and blackberry combination that contrasts both flavor and color.*

**2 cups fresh blackberries or 1 (12- or 16-oz.) pkg.**
  **thawed, frozen, unsweetened blackberries, drained**
**1/2 to 3/4 cup sugar**
**1/4 cup almond liqueur or orange juice**
**1/4 cup toasted sliced almonds, for garnish**

Crush blackberries or pulse in a food processor. Press through a strainer to remove seeds. Discard seeds and place blackberry pulp in a small saucepan; stir in sugar.

Cook over medium heat, stirring until sugar is dissolved. Remove from heat and stir in almond liqueur or orange juice. Serve warm or cold over fritters and garnish with almonds. Makes 2-1/4 cups.

### Variation

Omit blackberries and substitute an equal amount of raspberries, blueberries or mixed berries.

# Mocha-Hazelnut Pancakes

*For your next dinner party, serve these delightful small dessert pancakes as the final touch. Try topping them with the chocolate and marmalade sauces on the opposite page. These pancakes can be made ahead, covered and served at room temperature.*

**2 to 3 bread slices**
**3/4 cup coffee**
**1 cup coffee-flavored yogurt**
**2 eggs, separated**
**5 tablespoons sugar**
**1/2 cup all-purpose flour**
**2 tablespoons unsweetened cocoa powder**
**1 tablespoon baking powder**
**2/3 to 3/4 cup chopped toasted hazelnuts**
**2 tablespoons melted butter or margarine**

In a blender or food processor, process enough bread to make 1-1/2 cups fine crumbs. Place in a medium bowl and set aside. In a small bowl, combine coffee and coffee-flavored yogurt. Pour over crumbs and stir to combine thoroughly; let stand 10 minutes. Preheat a nonstick griddle or lightly oiled heavy skillet. Whip egg whites until stiff; set aside. Beat yolks and stir into crumb mixture. Stir in sugar, flour, cocoa powder, baking powder, hazelnuts and melted butter or margarine; mix together until blended. Fold in whipped egg whites.

Using preheated griddle or skillet, pour or spoon about 2 tablespoons batter for each pancake. Cook pancakes until bubbles appear and edges look slightly dry. Turn over and continue cooking until lightly browned. Serve with Chocolate-Mocha Sauce and Grand Marnier Sauce, opposite. Makes 20 to 24 pancakes.

# Chocolate-Mocha Sauce

*Treat yourself to a smooth and rich-tasting sauce.*

**1 cup semisweet chocolate chips**
**1/4 cup coffee**
**1/4 teaspoon ground cinnamon**
**6 tablespoons corn syrup**
**2 teaspoons butter or margarine**
**Chopped roasted hazelnuts**

In a small saucepan, heat all ingredients except nuts over low heat until chocolate is melted. Or place in a microwavable cup and cook on HIGH (100%) 1 to 1-1/2 minutes until chocolate chips soften. Remove and stir in some of the hazelnuts. Serve warm or at room temperature. Sprinkle with additional chopped hazelnuts. Makes about 1 cup.

# Grand Marnier Sauce

*Transform marmalade into a taste sensation by just adding two ingredients.*

**1/2 cup orange marmalade**
**1 tablespoon lemon juice**
**3 to 4 tablespoons Grand Marnier, Cointreau or**
**    orange juice**

In a small bowl, combine orange marmalade, lemon juice and Grand Marnier, Cointreau or orange juice. Stir well. If mixture is too stiff to drizzle, add a little more liqueur or juice. Makes about 3/4 cup.

# Double-Chocolate Oatmeal Pancakes

*This is for those of you who can never have too much chocolate.*

**1/2 cup oatmeal**
**1 cup all-purpose flour**
**2 tablespoons sugar**
**1 tablespoon baking powder**
**1 teaspoon baking soda**
**2 tablespoons unsweetened cocoa powder**
**1/2 cup egg substitute or 2 eggs**
**1-1/4 cups buttermilk**
**1 teaspoon vanilla extract**
**1/4 cup semisweet mini chocolate chips or chopped**
  **chocolate chips**

**Chocolate-flavored yogurt**

Preheat a nonstick griddle or lightly oiled heavy skillet. Combine all ingredients except chocolate chips and yogurt in a medium bowl, blender or food processor; blend briefly. Stir in chocolate chips.

Using preheated griddle or skillet, pour or spoon about 1/4 cup batter for each pancake. Cook pancakes until bubbles appear and edges look slightly dry. Turn over and continue cooking until lightly browned. Serve with dollops of chocolate-flavored yogurt and/or Brandy-Chocolate Sauce, opposite. Makes 14 to 16 pancakes.

# Brandy-Chocolate Sauce

*Whenever you have an urge for an almost sinful sauce, try this one.*

**2 tablespoons corn syrup**
**1/2 cup sugar**
**2 tablespoons unsweetened cocoa powder**
**1/4 cup water**
**1/4 cup brandy or 1 tablespoon brandy extract plus**
  **3 tablespoons orange juice**
**1 teaspoon vanilla extract**
**2 tablespoons butter or margarine**

In a small saucepan, combine corn syrup, sugar, cocoa powder and water. Cook, stirring occasionally, over medium heat about 5 minutes. Stir in brandy or brandy extract and orange juice, vanilla and butter or margarine. Serve warm or at room temperature. Makes about 1 cup.

## Variation

Substitute whipping cream for water and add 1/4 cup toasted chopped walnuts.

# Apricot-Chiffon Pancakes

*Bits of apricot in the pancakes reflect the fruit hidden under the meringue.*

**1 (32-oz.) can apricot halves, drained**
**1 cup all-purpose flour**
**1 tablespoon baking powder**
**1 tablespoon sugar**
**1 tablespoon oil**
**1 teaspoon rum extract**
**2 egg whites, beaten**

**Nutmeg Meringue, opposite**

Preheat a nonstick griddle or lightly oiled heavy skillet. Set aside 15 or 16 apricot halves. Combine remaining apricot halves, flour, baking powder, sugar, oil and rum extract in a blender or food processor; blend briefly to puree apricots. Pour into a medium bowl and fold in egg whites.

Using preheated griddle or skillet, pour or spoon about 1 tablespoon batter for each pancake. Cook pancakes until bubbles appear and edges look slightly dry. Turn over and continue cooking until lightly browned. Place pancakes in a single layer on a cookie sheet.

Preheat oven to 325F (165C). Prepare Nutmeg Meringue. Place a reserved apricot half cut-side down on each pancake. Top with Nutmeg Meringue. Bake in preheated oven 12 to 15 minutes or until golden brown. Remove and serve at once. Makes about 15 pancakes.

# *Nutmeg Meringue*

*Generally, meringue made with one egg white makes a topping for five pancakes.*

**3 egg whites**
**1/4 teaspoon cream of tartar**
**6 tablespoons sugar**
**1/4 teaspoon ground nutmeg**

Preheat oven to 325F (160C). In a large bowl, beat egg whites and cream of tartar until frothy. Continue beating while slowly adding sugar and nutmeg. Beat until stiff but still glossy. Spoon 1 heaping tablespoon meringue over each apricot half, covering it.

Bake in preheated oven 12 to 15 minutes or until golden brown.

# MOSTLY VEGETABLES

While savory or nonsweet recipes can contain a wide range of ingredients, I'm using mostly vegetables. A variety of herbs and spices accents rather different combinations. You can serve them as either a main dish or accompaniment.

How often do you end up with a small portion of leftover vegetables that are too good to throw out? Here are a variety of ways to put those bits and dabs to work for you. The results will be pleasing.

Keeping in mind that many of you are watching your fat intake, the fritters and cakes I offer are sautéed rather than deep-fried.

Most recipes can be made in minutes, but you can also make them ahead of time. Cover prepared fritters with foil or plastic wrap and refrigerate until needed. Warm by placing in a single layer on a cookie sheet and heat in a 350F (175C) oven for 15 minutes. Or you can reheat them in a microwave oven; lightly cover and briefly heat on HIGH (100%) until warm.

# Recipes

**Rockefeller Spinach Fritters**
*Herbed-Cheese Topping*

**Sweet-Potato Medley Fritters**
*Cucumber-Parsley Sauce*

**Southwestern Cherry-Chile Pancakes**
*Guacamole*

**East Indian Rice Fritters**
*Nectarine Chutney*

**Mexican Cheese & Chile Pancakes**
*Fresh Tomato Salsa*

**Mushroom Cake**
*Caponata*

**Spaghetti-Squash Fritters**
*Cheddar-Cheese Sauce*

**Tri-Pepper Pancakes**
*Tuna Sauce*

# *Rockefeller Spinach Fritters*

*Smoked oysters lend a unique flavor to this unusual treatment of spinach.*

**1 (10-oz.) pkg. thawed, frozen, chopped spinach, drained**
**1 egg**
**3 tablespoons all-purpose flour**
**1/4 cup chopped smoked oysters**
**2 shallots or 1 green onion, chopped**
**1/2 teaspoon garlic powder**
**1/2 teaspoon dry mustard**
**1/4 teaspoon ground nutmeg**
**Salt and pepper to taste**

**Oil for frying**

Squeeze or press out as much liquid as possible from thawed spinach. In a medium bowl, thoroughly combine all ingredients except oil. In a large heavy skillet, heat 1 to 2 tablespoons oil. Carefully spoon about 2 tablespoons spinach mixture into oil. Press lightly to form fritter. When edges begin to brown, turn and lightly press again and cook other side. Place on absorbent paper or paper towel. Cover to keep warm. If necessary, add more oil to skillet and continue cooking fritters. Serve with Herbed-Cheese Topping, opposite, or Hot Mustard Sauce, page 71. Makes about 8 fritters.

# *Herbed-Cheese Topping*

*Serving this simple topping at room temperature brings out its flavor.*

**1 (3-oz.) pkg. cream cheese, softened**
**1/4 cup plain yogurt**
**1 teaspoon garlic powder**
**1 teaspoon onion powder**
**1 tablespoon chopped fresh parsley**
**1/2 teaspoon dried-leaf tarragon**
**1 tablespoon chopped pimiento**
**Salt and pepper to taste**

In a small bowl, thoroughly combine all ingredients. Cover and refrigerate until needed. To serve, bring to room temperature. Stir and spoon over pancakes. Makes about 2/3 cup.

# Sweet-Potato Medley Fritters

*An unlikely flavor combination in a strikingly pretty fritter.*

**1 (8-oz.) raw sweet potato, peeled, shredded**
**1 carrot, peeled, shredded**
**1 tablespoon minced onion**
**2 eggs**
**1/4 cup all-purpose flour**
**3 tablespoons orange juice**
**2 teaspoons grated orange peel**
**2 tablespoons chopped fresh parsley**
**Salt and pepper to taste**

**Oil for frying**

In a medium bowl, thoroughly combine all ingredients except oil. In a large heavy skillet, heat 1 to 2 tablespoons oil. Carefully spoon about 2 tablespoons sweet-potato mixture into oil. Press lightly to form fritter. When edges begin to brown, turn and lightly press again and cook other side. Place on absorbent paper or paper towel. Cover to keep warm. If necessary, add more oil to skillet and continue cooking fritters. Serve with Cucumber-Parsley Sauce, opposite, or Citrus Sauce, page 31. Makes 10 to 12 fritters.

# *Cucumber-Parsley Sauce*

*A cool and refreshing sauce that goes well with most vegetable or seafood fritters.*

**1 cucumber, peeled, seeded, grated**
**2 tablespoons chopped fresh parsley**
**1/4 cup dairy sour cream or plain yogurt**
**1 teaspoon sugar**
**2 tablespoons vinegar**
**Salt and pepper to taste**

In a small bowl, combine all ingredients. Cover and refrigerate until needed. Stir and spoon over fritters. Makes about 3/4 cup.

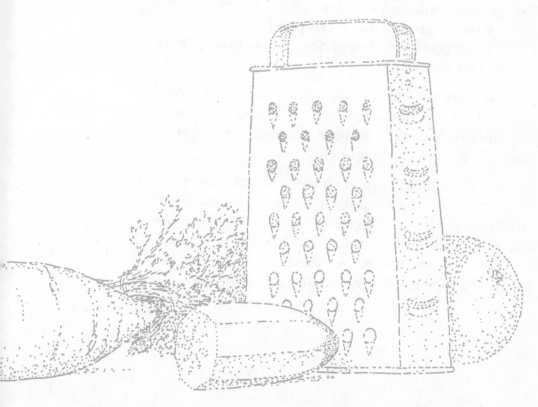

# Southwestern Cherry-Chile Pancakes

*A pleasing surprise to the palate. Your guests will be amazed to experience this unusual blend of sweet and hot. Adjust the amount of chiles to meet your own liking.*

3/4 cup all-purpose flour
1/2 cup cornmeal
1 teaspoon sugar
2 teaspoons baking powder
2 tablespoons oil
1 cup lowfat milk
1/4 teaspoon almond extract
1 to 2 roasted green chiles, chopped
1/2 cup chopped dried cherries or chopped, pitted,
    fresh tart cherries

Preheat a nonstick griddle or lightly oiled heavy skillet. Combine all ingredients except chiles and cherries, in a medium bowl, blender or food processor; mix until blended. Fold in chiles and cherries.

Using preheated griddle or skillet, pour or spoon about 1/4 cup batter for each pancake. Cook pancakes until bubbles appear and edges look slightly dry. Turn over and continue cooking until lightly browned. Top with Guacamole, opposite, grated cheddar cheese, or Fresh Tomato Salsa, page 59. Makes 10 to 12 pancakes.

# *Guacamole*

*Not just for tacos, guacamole gives a Mexican touch to any dish.*

**1 large ripe avocado, peeled, seeded, chopped**
**1 green onion, chopped**
**1 tablespoon lemon juice**
**1/2 tomato, seeded, chopped**
**1 small jalapeño chile pepper, seeded,**
  **chopped, if desired**

In a small bowl, combine all ingredients. Place a piece of plastic wrap on surface of mixture. This helps to maintain the color. Cover and refrigerate until needed. Makes about 2/3 cup.

# East Indian Rice Fritters

*Chutney is the perfect topping for these colorful fritters. Serve with slices of fresh melon and a cool drink.*

**1/4 cup dried currants**
**1/4 cup lime or lemon juice**
**2 cups cooked medium-grain rice**
**1/2 medium onion, chopped**
**2 eggs**
**1 medium apple, chopped**
**1/4 cup chopped peanuts**
**1 to 2 teaspoons curry powder**
**3 tablespoons cornstarch**
**Salt and pepper to taste**

**Oil for frying**

Soak currants in lime or lemon juice about 15 minutes. In a medium bowl, thoroughly combine all ingredients except oil. In a large heavy skillet, heat 1 to 2 tablespoons oil. Carefully spoon about 2 tablespoons rice mixture into oil. Press lightly to form fritter. When edges begin to brown, turn and lightly press again and cook other side. Place on absorbent paper or paper towel. Cover to keep warm. If necessary, add more oil to skillet and continue cooking fritters. Serve with Nectarine Chutney, opposite, Cucumber Relish, page 83 or watermelon pickles. Makes 10 to 12 fritters.

# *Nectarine Chutney*

*Make a double batch and always have chutney available to transform everyday foods such as cold cuts into something special. Peaches canned in natural juices make a perfect alternative to seasonal fresh nectarines.*

**1/4 cup chopped dates**
**1/2 cup dried currants or raisins**
**1/2 cup firmly packed brown sugar**
**1/2 medium onion, chopped**
**1 celery stalk, chopped**
**2 tablespoons chopped walnuts**
**1/2 cup cider vinegar**
**1 cinnamon stick**
**4 to 5 whole cloves**
**Dash red (cayenne) pepper**
**4 to 5 firm ripe nectarines, chopped**

In a large saucepan, combine all ingredients and bring to a boil. Reduce heat and simmer until fruit is tender, about 15 minutes. Cool and pour into a nonreactive container. Cover and refrigerate until needed. It may be stored up to 2 months. Makes about 2-3/4 cups.

# Mexican Cheese & Chile Pancakes

*A quick and easy way to satisfy that yearning for Mexican flavors.*

1/2 cup cornmeal
1/4 cup all-purpose or whole-wheat flour
1-1/2 teaspoons baking powder
3/4 cup evaporated milk
1 egg
1 tablespoon oil
3/4 cup shredded cheddar cheese
2 to 3 roasted green chiles, chopped
1 green onion, chopped
1/2 teaspoon dried-leaf oregano
Salt and pepper to taste

Preheat a nonstick griddle or lightly oiled heavy skillet. In a medium bowl, thoroughly combine all ingredients in the order they are listed.

Using preheated griddle or skillet, pour or spoon about 1/4 cup batter for each pancake. Cook pancakes until bubbles appear and edges look slightly dry. Turn over and continue cooking until lightly browned. Serve with Fresh Tomato Salsa, opposite, or Guacamole, page 55. Makes 10 to 12 pancakes.

# *Fresh Tomato Salsa*

*Luckily, we can get fresh tomatoes throughout the year. Use as many chiles as your taste buds allow.*

**3 ripe tomatoes, chopped**
**1/2 medium onion, chopped**
**1/4 green bell pepper, chopped**
**3 tablespoons chopped fresh cilantro**
**1 teaspoon chopped fresh parsley**
**1 garlic clove, minced**
**1 tablespoon lemon or lime juice**
**2 roasted green chiles, chopped**
**1 small jalapeño chile pepper, seeded,**
  **chopped, if desired**

In a small bowl, combine all ingredients. Cover and refrigerate until needed. Makes about 1-1/2 cups.

# Mushroom Cake

*Choose from two suggested toppings for this large skillet cake, or just enjoy with the broiled cheese.*

**3 tablespoons butter or oil**
**4 green onions, sliced (1/3 cup)**
**12 oz. fresh mushrooms, sliced (3 cups)**
**1/2 teaspoon dried-leaf thyme**
**1 egg, beaten**
**1/2 cup (4 oz.) herb-and-garlic-flavored cream cheese,**
  **softened, or plain yogurt**
**2 tablespoons cornstarch**
**1 tablespoon all-purpose flour**
**1 teaspoon soy sauce**
**Salt and pepper to taste**
**1/4 cup goat cheese or blue cheese, crumbled**

Preheat broiler. In a medium ovenproof skillet, heat butter or oil. Sauté onions, mushrooms and thyme over medium heat until softened; set aside. In a large bowl, beat together egg, cheese or yogurt, cornstarch, flour and soy sauce until well blended. Season with salt and pepper to taste. Carefully pour egg mixture over onions and mushrooms in skillet.

Cover and cook over medium heat until edges begin to brown, about 5 minutes. Crumble goat cheese or blue cheese over cake. Place skillet under broiler 3 to 4 minutes or until cheese is melted and top is speckled. Slide cake onto a warm serving plate. Cut into wedges. Serve with Caponata, opposite, or Cranberry-Orange Sauce, page 77. Makes 6 to 8 servings.

# *Caponata*

*A versatile accompaniment that can be served hot or at room temperature.*

**1/4 cup olive oil**
**1 onion, chopped**
**2 garlic cloves, minced**
**1 (1-lb.) eggplant, unpeeled, cut into 1-inch cubes**
**1 cup chopped celery**
**2 tomatoes, peeled, chopped**
**1 cup tomato sauce**
**2 tablespoons capers**
**1/2 cup sliced pimiento-stuffed olives**
**2 tablespoons red-wine vinegar**
**2 tablespoons tomato juice**
**1 tablespoon chopped fresh basil**
**Salt and pepper to taste**

In a large skillet, heat oil. Sauté onion and garlic over medium heat until softened. Add eggplant and celery; stir until browned. Add remaining ingredients. Reduce heat and simmer about 15 minutes or until vegetables are tender. Serve warm or chilled. Cover and refrigerate until needed. It may be stored up to 2 weeks. Makes 6 to 8 servings.

# Spaghetti-Squash Fritters

*Capers and bacon add interest to the mild-flavored spaghetti squash. Chopped ham can be substituted for the bacon.*

**2 cups cooked spaghetti squash, pulled into strands**
**2 bacon slices, cooked, crumbled**
**2 tablespoons cornstarch**
**1 tablespoon chopped chives**
**1 tablespoon capers**
**1/2 teaspoon ground nutmeg**

**Oil for frying**

Cut spaghetti-squash strands into 2- to 3-inch lengths. In a medium bowl, beat egg. Add remaining ingredients and thoroughly combine.

In a large heavy skillet, heat 1 to 2 tablespoons oil. Carefully spoon about 2 tablespoons squash mixture into oil. Press lightly to form fritter. When edges begin to brown, turn and lightly press again and cook other side. Place on absorbent paper or paper towel. If necessary, add more oil to skillet and continue making fritters. Cover and keep warm. Serve with Cheddar-Cheese Sauce, opposite, Italian Tomato Sauce, page 112, or grated Romano cheese. Makes 10 to 12 fritters.

**Variation**

Omit spaghetti squash and substitute grated raw zucchini. Omit bacon and add 3 tablespoons chopped sun-dried tomatoes.

# *Cheddar-Cheese Sauce*

*For a milder flavor, use Tillamook or longhorn cheese rather than cheddar.*

**2 tablespoons butter**
**2 tablespoons all-purpose flour**
**1 cup chicken broth**
**1/2 cup evaporated milk**
**1/2 teaspoon dry mustard**
**1/2 cup grated sharp cheddar cheese**
**1 tablespoon chopped chives**
**1 tablespoon chopped pimiento**
**Salt and pepper to taste**

In a medium saucepan, melt butter and stir in flour. Stirring constantly, slowly blend in broth and milk. Continue stirring and cook until sauce has thickened and is smooth. Remove from heat; stir in remaining ingredients. Makes about 2 cups.

# Tri-Pepper Pancakes

*Many of the picture-perfect yellow and orange bell peppers are grown in Holland and shipped world-wide.*

**2 tablespoons olive oil**
**1/2 medium onion, chopped**
**1 garlic clove, minced**
**1 each red, green and yellow bell peppers,**
  **seeded, chopped**
**1 egg**
**1/3 cup plain yogurt**
**1/4 cup all-purpose flour**
**1/2 teaspoon paprika**
**1 teaspoon dried-leaf oregano**
**Salt and pepper to taste**

Preheat a nonstick griddle or lightly oiled heavy skillet. In a medium skillet, heat oil. Sauté onion, garlic and peppers over medium heat about 2 minutes; set aside to cool.

In a medium bowl, beat together egg, yogurt, flour, paprika, oregano, salt and pepper. Stir in pepper mixture.

Using preheated griddle or skillet, pour or spoon about 1/4 cup batter for each pancake. Press lightly. When edges begin to brown, turn and lightly press again and cook other side. Place on absorbent paper or paper towel. Cover and keep warm. Serve with Tuna Sauce, opposite, Marinara Sauce, page 81, or commercial spaghetti sauce. Makes 12 to 14 pancakes.

# *Tuna Sauce*

*Italians call this refreshing tuna sauce* tonnato. *No cooking required, and your blender does the work.*

**1 (6-1/2-oz.) can oil-packed tuna, drained**
**2 tablespoons fresh lemon juice**
**1/2 cup olive oil**
**1/4 cup chopped walnuts**
**2 anchovy fillets**
**1/2 cup mayonnaise**
**1 tablespoon chopped fresh parsley**

**2 tablespoons capers, if desired**

In a food processor or blender, combine all ingredients, except capers. Process until well combined. Cover and refrigerate until needed. Spoon into a serving bowl. Spoon sauce over pancakes and sprinkle with capers, if desired. Makes about 1-1/2 cups.

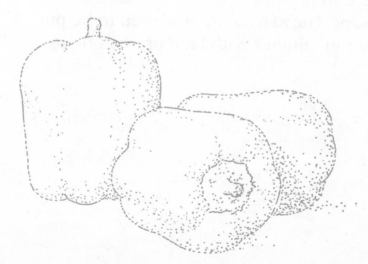

# SAVORY PANCAKES & TOPPINGS

The nonsweet savory pancakes and toppings in this chapter are ideal for quick and tasty weekend lunches or light suppers. If you want to add interest to a pancake lunch, try serving both the suggested sauces or toppings with the pancakes and add a salad or vegetable dish. Fresh fruit will round off your light meal perfectly.

Most of these pancakes use at least one leftover item such as roast beef or cooked chicken, so no special trip to the store is necessary. The sauces are designed to be put together in minutes with little or no cooking.

# Recipes

## Shrimp Fritters
*Pineapple Sweet & Sour Sauce*

## Ham & Leek Fritters
*Hot Mustard Sauce*

## Fish Cakes
*Tarragon-Mustard Sauce*

## Maryland Crab Cakes
*Spinach-Nutmeg Sauce*

## Turkey Cakes
*Cranberry-Orange Sauce*

## Curried Onion & Beef Cakes
*Creamed-Vegetable Sauce*

## Italian Sausage & Corn Cakes
*Marinara Sauce*

## Chicken-Teriyaki Fritters
*Cucumber Relish*

# Shrimp Fritters

*Chinese spices add interest to the shrimp, while a sweet-and-sour sauce complements the Oriental flavor combination.*

**2 tablespoons oil**
**1/4 medium onion, chopped**
**1 garlic clove, minced**
**2 teaspoons grated fresh ginger**
**1 egg**
**3 oz. cream cheese, softened**
**3 tablespoons cornstarch**
**3/4 teaspoon Chinese five-spice powder**
**1/4 cup peas**
**1 cup cooked, peeled, deveined cocktail shrimp**
**Salt and pepper to taste**

**Oil for frying**

In a medium skillet, heat 2 tablespoons oil. Sauté onion, garlic and ginger over medium heat until softened; set aside. In a medium bowl, beat together egg, cream cheese, cornstarch and five-spice powder. Stir in onion mixture, peas and shrimp. Season with salt and pepper to taste.

In a large heavy skillet, heat 1 to 2 tablespoons oil. Carefully spoon about 2 tablespoons shrimp mixture into oil. Press lightly to form fritter. When edges begin to brown, turn and lightly press again and cook other side. Place on absorbent paper or paper towel. Cover and keep warm. If necessary, add more oil to skillet and continue cooking fritters. Serve with Pineapple Sweet & Sour Sauce, opposite, or hoisin sauce. Makes 10 to 12 fritters.

# *Pineapple Sweet & Sour Sauce*

*For added color and flavor, include a quarter of a green bell pepper cut into one-inch squares when you add the pineapple.*

**1 (8-oz.) can pineapple chunks**
**1 tablespoon cornstarch**
**1 tablespoon soy sauce**
**1 tablespoon sugar**
**1 tablespoon rice vinegar or cider vinegar**
**1 teaspoon catsup**

Drain pineapple, reserving juice; set aside. In a small saucepan, combine cornstarch, soy sauce and sugar. Stir in vinegar and catsup. If necessary, add water to reserved pineapple juice to make 3/4 cup. Add to saucepan. Cook, stirring occasionally, until thickened and clear. Add pineapple and stir to coat. Serve warm. Makes about 1-1/2 cups.

# Ham & Leek Fritters

*Ham is a natural to pair with leeks, those large but mild-flavored members of the onion family.*

**2 leeks, trimmed**
**2 tablespoons butter**
**2 eggs**
**1/4 cup cottage cheese**
**1/4 cup shredded Gruyère cheese**
**1 tablespoon melted butter or oil**
**1/4 cup all-purpose flour**
**1 cup chopped ham**
**1/4 teaspoon dry mustard**
**1/4 teaspoon paprika**

**Oil for frying**

Prepare leeks by cutting each one lengthwise and rinsing under running water so dirt between layers is washed away. Finely chop leeks. In a medium skillet, heat 2 tablespoons butter. Sauté leeks over medium-low heat until softened. In a medium bowl, beat together eggs, cottage cheese, Gruyère cheese and 1 tablespoon melted butter or oil. Stir in flour, leeks, ham, mustard and paprika.

In a large heavy skillet, heat 1 to 2 tablespoons oil. Carefully spoon about 1/4 cup ham mixture into oil. Press lightly to form fritter. When edges begin to brown, turn and lightly press again and cook other side. Place on absorbent paper or paper towel. Cover and keep warm. If necessary, add more oil to skillet and continue cooking fritters. Serve with Hot Mustard Sauce, opposite, or Cranberry-Orange Sauce, page 77. Makes 8 to 9 fritters.

# Hot Mustard Sauce

*Tiny mustard seeds are ground into powder and provide us with a robust flavoring.*

**1 tablespoon hot dry mustard**
**3 tablespoons hot water**
**2 tablespoons butter or oil**
**2 tablespoons all-purpose flour**
**1 cup milk**
**1 egg yolk, beaten**
**1 teaspoon vinegar**
**Salt and pepper to taste**

In a cup, blend together mustard and hot water; set aside.

In a medium skillet, heat butter or oil over medium heat. Stir in flour and blend making a smooth paste. Stirring constantly, gradually add milk and reserved mustard mixture. Continue stirring and blend in egg yolk and vinegar. Sauce should be thick and smooth. Season with salt and pepper to taste. Serve warm. Makes about 1-1/2 cups.

# *Fish Cakes*

*You can enjoy these cakes without a sauce. Or, sprinkle with a dash of malt vinegar or bottled hot sauce.*

**1/2 cup cubed cooked potato**
**1-1/2 cups flaked cooked cod, sole or haddock**
**1/4 cup all-purpose flour or cornstarch**
**2 eggs**
**1/4 cup beer**
**1/2 teaspoon paprika**
**1 teaspoon dry mustard**
**1/2 teaspoon dried-leaf oregano**
**1/2 cup fresh bread crumbs**
**Salt and pepper to taste**

**Oil for frying**

In a food processor or blender, process all ingredients briefly until combined.

In a large heavy skillet, heat 1 to 2 tablespoons oil. Carefully spoon about 2 tablespoons fish mixture into oil. Press lightly to form cake. When edges begin to brown, turn and lightly press again and cook other side. Place on absorbent paper or paper towel. If necessary, add more oil to skillet and continue cooking cakes. Cover and keep warm. Serve with Tarragon Sauce, opposite, or Cold Beet Relish, page 116. Makes 14 to 16 cakes.

# *Tarragon-Mustard Sauce*

*No cooking is required to make this satisfying cold sauce.*

**1/2 cup plain yogurt**
**1/2 cup mayonnaise**
**1 green onion, chopped**
**2 tablespoons prepared Dijon mustard**
**2 tablespoons tarragon-flavored vinegar**
**1 tablespoon fresh tarragon leaves or 1 teaspoon**
  **dried-leaf tarragon**
**2 teaspoons capers, if desired**
**1 teaspoon curry powder, if desired**

In a small bowl, combine yogurt, mayonnaise and onion. Stir in mustard, vinegar, tarragon, capers and curry powder, if desired. Cover and refrigerate until needed. Makes about 1-1/4 cups.

# *Maryland Crab Cakes*

*When using canned crab, pat with paper towel after draining to remove any excess liquid.*

**1 egg**
**1/2 cup mayonnaise**
**1/2 cup fresh bread crumbs**
**1 green onion, chopped**
**1 teaspoon Worcestershire sauce**
**1 tablespoon lemon juice**
**1 tablespoon chopped pimientos**
**1/4 teaspoon dry mustard**
**1/4 teaspoon celery salt**
**1/4 teaspoon dried-leaf thyme**
**1 tablespoon capers**
**3/4 lb. cooked crab meat or 2 (6-oz.) cans crab, drained**

**Oil for frying**

In a large bowl, beat egg and mayonnaise. Thoroughly mix in bread crumbs. Stir in remaining ingredients except oil. Shape crab mixture into 6 to 8 patties. Cover and refrigerate about 45 minutes.

In a large heavy skillet, heat 1 to 2 tablespoons oil. Add crab cakes and cook each side until golden brown. Place on absorbent paper or paper towel. Cover and keep warm. If necessary, add more oil to skillet and continue cooking cakes. Serve with Spinach-Nutmeg Sauce, opposite, Cold Chili Sauce, page 116, or salsa. Makes 6 to 8 cakes.

# *Spinach-Nutmeg Sauce*

*Freshly grated nutmeg gives the very best flavor, but ground nutmeg is certainly a good substitute.*

**1 (10-oz.) pkg. thawed, frozen, chopped spinach, drained**
**2 tablespoons butter or margarine**
**2 tablespoons all-purpose flour**
**1/4 cup evaporated milk mixed with 1/4 cup water**
**1/2 cup vermouth or chicken broth**
**1 tablespoon chopped pimiento**
**1/2 teaspoon ground nutmeg**

Squeeze or press out as much liquid as possible from thawed spinach. Finely chop spinach; set aside.

In a medium saucepan, melt butter or margarine and blend in flour. Stirring constantly, slowly add milk. Cook until thickened and smooth. Stir in vermouth or chicken broth, pimiento and nutmeg; cook until heated. Serve warm. Makes about 2-1/2 cups.

# Turkey Cakes

*After we've enjoyed roast turkey, we're always looking for new ways to serve the leftover meat. Here is one way you may not have tried before.*

**1 egg**
**1 tablespoon oil**
**1/2 cup all-purpose flour**
**1/2 cup turkey broth or milk**
**1/4 teaspoon poultry seasoning**
**2 tablespoons finely chopped celery**
**1/4 cup dried currants**
**1 green onion, chopped**
**1-1/4 cups finely chopped cooked turkey or chicken**

**Oil for frying**

In a medium bowl, beat egg and 1 tablespoon oil together. Stir in remaining ingredients except oil. Shape turkey mixture into 8 to 10 patties. Cover and refrigerate about 45 minutes.

In a large heavy skillet, heat 1 to 2 tablespoons oil. Add turkey cakes and cook each side until golden brown. Place on absorbent paper or paper towel. Cover and keep warm. If necessary, add more oil to skillet and continue cooking cakes. Serve with Cranberry-Orange Sauce, opposite, Plum Relish, page 113, or Lemony Walnut Sauce, page 19. Makes 8 to 10 cakes.

# Cranberry-Orange Sauce

*Buy several packages of fresh cranberrries and freeze them for use year-round. They are great to serve during warm summer months.*

**1 (16-oz.) bag fresh cranberries**
**1/2 cup firmly packed brown sugar**
**1/3 cup orange-juice concentrate**
**1/2 cup water**
**1/3 cup orange marmalade**
**1/4 cup chopped pistachios**

**Additional chopped pistachios**

In a large saucepan, combine cranberries, sugar, orange juice and water. Cook over medium heat, stirring occasionally, until cranberry skins burst. Stir in marmalade and 1/4 cup pistachios; continue cooking until sauce has slightly thickened. Pour into a serving bowl to cool. Sprinkle top with additional pistachios. Serve warm or chilled. Makes about 3 cups.

# Curried Onion & Beef Cakes

*Let your palate guide you on the amount of curry powder to use.*

**1 tablespoon oil**
**2 small onions, finely chopped**
**1 teaspoon sugar**
**1 cup shredded roast beef**
**1 egg**
**2 to 3 teaspoons curry powder**
**2 tablespoons plain yogurt**
**1/4 cup all-purpose flour**
**1/4 teaspoon paprika**
**Salt and pepper to taste**

In a medium skillet, heat oil over medium heat. Add onions, stirring until limp. Sprinkle with sugar and mix together. Reduce heat to simmer; cover and cook 3 to 4 minutes. Stir in beef. Remove from heat and cool.

In a medium bowl, food processor or blender, combine remaining ingredients; process until well combined. Stir in onion mixture.

Preheat a nonstick griddle or lightly oiled heavy skillet. Using preheated griddle or skillet, carefully spoon on about 2 tablespoons beef mixture for each cake. Press lightly to form cakes. When edges begin to brown, turn and lightly press again and cook other side. Place on absorbent paper or paper towel. Serve with Creamed-Vegetable Sauce, opposite, Orange-Raisin Sauce, page 11, or Cucumber Relish, page 83. Makes 8 to 10 cakes.

# Creamed-Vegetable Sauce

*Choose your favorite vegetables. I like to make colorful combinations such as carrots, peas, cauliflower and broccoli.*

**2 tablespoons butter**
**2 tablespoons all-purpose flour**
**1 cup milk**
**1 teaspoon Worcestershire sauce, if desired**
**1-1/2 cups cooked vegetables**
**Dash dried-leaf thyme**
**Dash paprika**
**Salt and pepper to taste**

In a small saucepan, melt butter over medium heat. Stir in flour. Slowly stir in milk; cook stirring, until mixture is thickened and smooth. Stir in Worcestershire sauce, if desired, vegetables, thyme and paprika. Season with salt and pepper to taste. Makes about 2-3/4 cups.

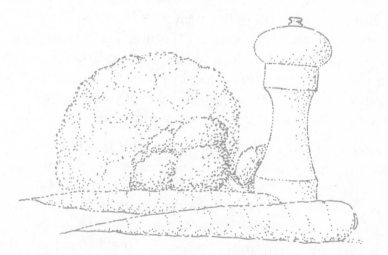

# *Italian Sausage & Corn Cakes*

*Almost a meal by itself, this light entrée only needs a fresh green salad. Or, serve for breakfast along with grilled tomatoes sprinkled with basil.*

**2 Italian sausages**
**1-3/4 cups cooked corn (fresh, frozen or canned)**
**1 egg**
**1/2 cup milk**
**2 teaspoons baking powder**
**1/4 cup corn meal**
**3/4 cup all-purpose flour**
**2 tablespoons melted butter or margarine**
**1/4 teaspoon paprika**
**2 teaspoons chopped fresh basil or 1/2 teaspoon**
  **dried-leaf oregano**
**2 green onions, chopped**

**Oil for frying**

Remove casing from sausage; cook in a small skillet over medium heat, breaking up meat as it browns. Drain excess fat; set sausage aside. Combine 1 cup corn, egg. milk, baking powder, corn meal, flour and butter or margarine in a blender or food processor. Blend briefly or pulse food processor to mix but not purée. Pour into a medium bowl. Stir in remaining ingredients.

In a large heavy skillet, heat 1 to 2 tablespoons oil. Carefully spoon about 1/4 cup sausage mixture into oil. Press lightly to form cake. When edges begin to brown, turn and lightly press again and cook other side. Place on absorbent paper or paper towel. Cover to keep warm. Top with Marinara Sauce, opposite, and Parmesan cheese. Makes 12 cakes.

# *Marinara Sauce*

*This Italian classic is a great basic sauce. I make a double batch and freeze some in small freezer bags.*

**2 tablespoons olive oil**
**1 garlic clove, minced**
**1 small onion, chopped**
**1 (14-oz.) can tomatoes**
**1 (8-oz.) can tomato sauce**
**1 tablespoon chopped fresh parsley**
**1/4 teaspoon dried-leaf oregano**
**1 tablespoon chopped fresh basil or 1-1/2 teaspoons**
  **dried-leaf basil**
**Dash sugar**
**Salt and pepper to taste**

In a small skillet, heat oil. Add garlic and onion; sauté briefly over medium heat until softened. Add remaining ingredients and bring to a boil. Reduce heat and simmer about 15 minutes. Serve warm. Makes about 2 cups.

# Chicken-Teriyaki Fritters

*Give an Oriental touch to leftover chicken.*

1/4 teaspoon garlic powder
2 tablespoons soy sauce
2 teaspoons sugar
1 tablespoon rice vinegar or cider vinegar
1-1/2 cups finely chopped cooked chicken
1 egg
1/2 cup all-purpose flour
1 teaspoon baking powder
1/3 cup chicken broth
1 teaspoon sesame oil

Oil for frying

In a small bowl, combine garlic powder, soy sauce, sugar and vinegar. Add chicken and toss to coat. Set aside to marinate about 5 minutes.

In a medium bowl, beat together egg, flour, baking powder, broth and sesame oil. Stir in chicken and mix thoroughly.

In a large heavy skillet, heat 1 to 2 tablespoons oil. Carefully spoon about 2 tablespoons chicken mixture into oil. Press lightly to form fritter. When edges begin to brown, turn and lightly press again and cook other side. Place on absorbent paper or paper towel. Cover to keep warm. If necessary, add oil to skillet and continue cooking fritters. Serve with Cucumber Relish, opposite, Hot Mustard Sauce, page 71 or teriyaki sauce. Makes 8 or 9 fritters.

# *Cucumber Relish*

*Cool cucumbers and crisp radishes provide the perfect contrast for tasty Oriental chicken fritters.*

**1 cucumber**
**2 tablespoons rice vinegar or cider vinegar**
**2 tablespoons lemon juice**
**1 to 2 tablespoons sugar**
**Salt and pepper to taste**
**4 or 5 radishes, thinly sliced**
**1 teaspoon toasted sesame seeds**

Peel cucumber and cut long shreds the length of the cucumber using a potato peeler or finely chop. Set aside in a sieve to drain about 20 minutes.

In a small bowl, stir together vinegar, lemon juice and sugar until sugar is dissolved. Add cucumber, radishes and salt and pepper to taste. Cover and refrigerate until needed. To serve, drain excess liquid, if desired, and sprinkle with sesame seeds. Makes about 1-1/2 cups.

# INTERNATIONAL PANCAKES & FRITTERS

Pancakes from countries around the world are recognized by a variety of names. French *crêpes,* Russian *blini,* the Italian *frittata,* and Jewish *latkes* are but a few of many you may know. You'll find both sweet and savory ones in this chapter.

Spain claims a potato pancake and calls it a *tortilla.* This is not to be confused with the flat flour or cornmeal Mexican tortilla, a staple used in a myriad of ways. And of course the Chinese have Mandarin pancakes.

# Recipes

Blini
*Blini Toppings*

Blintzes
*Cottage-Cheese Filling*

Savory Crêpes

Chicken-Filled Crêpes

Seafood-Filled Crêpes

Vegetable-Filled Crêpes

Cannelloni Pancakes

Chicken & Ham Filled Cannelloni

Manicotti

Cheese Filled Manicotti

Mandarin Pancakes
*Barbecued-Meat Filling*

Broiled Garlic Shrimp

Potato Latkes
*Apple Chutney*

Macaroni Frittata
*Creamy Spinach & Walnut Pesto*

Drop Scones
*Apricot-Almond Butter*

Highland Pancakes
*Maple Sauce*

Dessert Crêpes
*Dessert-Crêpe Fillings*

# *Blini*

*These delicate buckwheat pancakes originally came from Russia, but are now served in many countries. Try several different toppings.*

**3 cups milk**
**1 (1/4-oz.) pkg. active dry yeast (1 tablespoon)**
**2 teaspoons sugar**
**2 egg yolks, beaten**
**1/2 teaspoon salt**
**1 cup buckwheat flour**
**1-1/2 cups all-purpose flour**
**3 tablespoons melted butter or margarine**
**2 egg whites**

Warm milk to lukewarm and pour into a large bowl. Remove 1/4 cup warm milk to a cup; add yeast and sugar, stirring to dissolve. Set aside about 5 minutes.

Stir beaten yolks, salt and both types of flour into milk in bowl. Add yeast mixture. Beat until smooth. Cover and place in a warm area; let rise until doubled in bulk, about 2 hours.

Stir in melted butter or margarine. In a medium bowl, beat egg whites until stiff. Fold into batter just before cooking.

Preheat a nonstick griddle or lightly oiled heavy skillet. Using preheated griddle or skillet, pour or spoon about 2 tablespoons batter for each blin. Cook over medium heat until bubbles appear and edges look slightly dry. Turn over and continue cooking until lightly browned. Serve with toppings, opposite, or flavored fruit butters, pages 114 and 115. Makes about 24 blini.

# Blini Toppings

*For a special occasion, set out bowls of toppings buffet-style. Serve the blini on a large platter and let guests choose their own combination of toppings.*

In separate bowls, offer any of the following toppings.

**caviar**
**melted butter**
**chutney**
**chopped hard-cooked eggs**
**pickled herring**
**chopped onion**
**smoked oysters**
**thinly sliced smoked salmon**
**grilled sausage**
**sour cream**

# Blintzes

*These delightful cheese-filled bundles have become very popular for brunch. Serve with a variety of toppings.*

**1 cup all-purpose flour**
**3 eggs**
**1-1/2 cups milk**
**2 tablespoons sugar**
**1 tablesoon melted butter**
**1 teaspoon vanilla extract**

**Oil for frying**

In a blender, food processor or medium bowl, combine flour, eggs, milk, sugar, butter and vanilla. Lightly brush a crêpe pan or 6- to 7-inch skillet with oil. Pour about 2 tablespoons batter into pan, immediately tilt pan so batter covers the bottom. Cook until surface looks dry and edges are lacy and brown. Flip pancake onto a warm plate. Only one side needs to be cooked. Fill with Cottage-Cheese Filling, opposite. Makes about 12 blintzes.

# Cottage-Cheese Filling

*For a smoother filling, combine all ingredients, except raisins, in a food processor.*

**2 cups small-curd cottage cheese**
**1/2 cup dairy sour cream**
**3 tablespoons sugar**
**1 teaspoon vanilla extract**
**1 tablespoon grated lemon or orange peel**
**1/2 cup raisins, if desired**

**Butter**
**Dairy sour cream**
**Strawberry preserves**

In a small bowl, thoroughly combine cottage cheese, sour cream and sugar. Stir in vanilla, lemon or orange peel and raisins, if desired. Cover and set aside.

To fill blintzes, place a heaping tablespoon of filling in the center of the browned side; fold over top and bottom edges, then sides, making a square package. Brush a skillet with melted butter, add filled blintzes and gently fry over medium heat until golden. Turn to brown both sides, being careful not to let them burn. Serve hot or place in a baking dish.

At this point, blintzes can be covered and refrigerated for several days. Before serving, warm in a 350F (175C) oven about 20 minutes until heated.

Serve warm with sour cream and strawberry preserves, or fresh blueberries or strawberries.

**Tip:** In Tel Aviv, little restaurants and cafés specialize in blintzes. There they offer as many as 20 different toppings.

# Savory Crêpes

*What a great way to make leftovers into a party dish.*

**2 cups all-purpose flour**
**2 eggs**
**2-1/2 cups milk**
**1/4 teaspoon salt**
**2 tablespoons melted butter or oil**
**1 teaspoon dried-leaf parsley, basil or thyme, if desired**

Combine all ingredients in a medium bowl, blender or food processor; mix until blended. Let batter rest about 30 minutes.

Lightly brush a crêpe pan or 6- to 7-inch skillet with oil. Pour about 2 tablespoons batter into pan, immediately tilt pan so batter covers the bottom. Cook until surface looks dry and edges are lacy and brown. Turn and brown other side, this takes about 5 seconds; do not burn. Remove from pan and stack with waxed paper between crêpes. Repeat until all batter is used. Fill with Chicken Filling, opposite, Seafood Filling, page 92, or Vegetarian Filling, page 93. Makes 8 to 10 crêpes.

# Chicken-Filled Crêpes

*A wonderful entrée to make ahead. Cover and refrigerate or freeze the filling until needed.*

**2 tablespoons oil**
**2 green onions, chopped**
**2 tablespoons all-purpose flour**
**1/2 cup chicken broth**
**1/2 cup milk**
**1/2 cup dairy sour cream**
**1/4 cup orange juice**
**1/4 teaspoon paprika**
**1 cup chopped cooked chicken**
**1/2 cup thawed frozen peas**
**1/4 cup chopped cashews**
**Salt and pepper to taste**
**Savory Crêpes, opposite**
**1 (6-oz.) can mandarin oranges, drained**

In a medium skillet, heat oil. Add onions and sauté over medium heat until softened. Blend in flour. Add broth and milk, stirring until sauce is thickened. Stir in sour cream, orange juice, paprika, chicken, peas and cashews. Season with salt and pepper to taste.

Fill and roll crêpes, reserving 1/2 cup sauce. In a shallow baking dish, arrange filled crêpes seam-side down in a single layer. Pour reserved sauce over crêpes, top with mandarin oranges. Cover and bake in a 350F (175C) oven 15 to 20 minutes. Makes 8 to 10 crêpes.

## Variation

Omit peas, cashews and oranges. Add 1/2 cup sliced fresh mushrooms, 1 cup chopped blanched spinach and 1/2 cup shredded Swiss cheese. Use remaining ingredients listed in recipe.

# Seafood-Filled Crêpes

*Scallops or firm white fish can be added or substituted for the crab or shrimp.*

**2 tablespoons butter or oil**
**2 green onions, chopped**
**1/2 cup chopped mushrooms**
**2 tablespoons all-purpose flour**
**1/2 cup plain yogurt**
**1/4 cup vermouth or white wine**
**1 small tomato, peeled, seeded, chopped**
**1 cup chopped cooked crab or shrimp**
**2 teaspoons dried-leaf tarragon**
**Salt and pepper to taste**
**Savory Crêpes, page 90**
**1/2 cup shredded Gruyère or Swiss cheese**

In a medium skillet, heat butter or oil. Add onions and mushrooms; sauté over medium heat until softened. Blend in flour and yogurt. Stir in vermouth or white wine until mixture is thickened and smooth. Add tomato, crab or shrimp and tarragon, stir until heated. Season with salt and pepper to taste.

Fill and roll crêpes, reserving about 1/2 cup sauce. In a shallow baking dish, arrange filled crêpes seam-side down in a single layer. Pour reserved sauce down center of crêpes, top with shredded cheese. Cover and bake in a 350F (175C) oven 15 to 20 minutes. Makes 8 to 10 crêpes.

# Vegetable-Filled Crêpes

*A colorful filling proves to be a pleasure to the eye as well as the taste.*

**2 tablespoons butter or oil**
**1 small onion, chopped**
**1/4 cup chopped green bell pepper**
**1/4 cup chopped celery**
**1/2 cup sliced fresh mushrooms**
**1/4 cup thawed frozen peas**
**1 large tomato, peeled, seeded, chopped**
**1/2 teaspoon dried-leaf basil**
**1/2 teaspoon dried-leaf oregano**
**Salt and pepper to taste**
**Savory Crêpes, page 90**
**1/2 cup Monterey Jack cheese**
**Additional Monterey Jack cheese**

In a medium skillet, heat butter or oil. Add onion, green bell pepper and celery; sauté over medium heat until softened. Add mushrooms and peas; stir-fry about 2 minutes. Add tomato, basil, oregano and salt and pepper to taste.

Using about 2 tablespoons filling for each crêpe, fill and roll crêpes sprinkling some cheese over filling in each. In a shallow baking dish, arrange filled crêpes seam-side down in a single layer. Sprinkle with additional cheese and bake in a 350F (175C) oven about 20 minutes or until cheese melts. Makes 8 to 10 crêpes.

# *Cannelloni Pancakes*

*A wonderful entrée for family or company.*

**3 eggs**
**3/4 cup water**
**3/4 cup all-purpose flour**
**2 tablespoons oil**
**1/4 teaspoon salt, if desired**

Combine all ingredients in a medium bowl, blender or food processor; mix until blended. Let batter rest about 30 minutes.

Lightly brush a crêpe pan or 6- to 7-inch skillet with oil. Pour about 2 tablespoons batter into pan, immediately tilt pan so batter covers the bottom. Cook until surface is dry and edges are lacy and brown. Only one side needs to be cooked.

Place pancake on a dish to cool. Stack with waxed paper between pancakes. Fill with Chicken & Ham Cannelloni Filling, opposite, or Broiled Garlic Shrimp, page 99, topped with Cheddar-Cheese Sauce, page 63. Makes 24 to 26 pancakes.

# Chicken-&-Ham-Filled Cannelloni

*This filling combines chicken and ham. You can substitute cooked veal roast for the ham.*

**1 tablespoon olive oil**
**1 small onion, chopped**
**1 garlic clove, minced**
**2 cups chopped cooked chicken**
**1 cup chopped cooked ham or roast pork**
**1 cup ricotta cheese**
**1 (10-oz.) pkg. thawed, frozen, chopped spinach,**
  **drained**
**2 eggs**
**1/2 cup grated Parmesan cheese**
**1/4 teaspoon dried-leaf basil**
**1 tablespoon chopped fresh parsley**
**Salt and pepper to taste**
**Dash nutmeg**
**Cannelloni Pancakes, opposite**

**White Sauce, page 112**
**Grated mozzarella cheese**

In a medium skillet, heat oil; add onion and garlic. Sauté over medium heat until softened; set aside. In a food processor or meat grinder, combine chicken, ham or pork, ricotta cheese, spinach and reserved onion mixture. Stir in remaining ingredients except White Sauce and mozzarella cheese.

Spoon about 1/4 cup filling down center of each pancake. Roll and place seam-side down in a shallow baking dish. Spoon White Sauce down the center and sprinkle with mozzarella cheese. Bake in a 350F (175C) oven about 20 minutes. Makes 24 to 26 pancakes.

# *Manicotti*

*Another Italian favorite that has a simple but delicious cheese filling. A great dish for your vegetarian friends.*

**4 eggs**
**1-1/2 cups water**
**1-1/2 cups all-purpose flour**
**2 tablespoons oil**
**1/4 teaspoon salt, if desired**

Combine all ingredients in a medium bowl, blender or food processor; mix until blended. Let batter rest about 30 minutes.

Lightly brush a crêpe pan or 6- to 7-inch skillet with oil. Pour about 2 tablespoons batter into pan, immediately tilt pan so batter covers the bottom. Cook until surface is dry and edges are lacy and brown. Only 1 side needs to be cooked. Place pancake on a dish to cool. Stack with waxed paper between pancakes.

Fill with Manicotti Cheese Filling, opposite, and top with Italian Tomato Sauce, page 112, Marinara Sauce, page 81, or Creamy Spinach & Walnut Pesto, page 103. Makes 28 to 30 pancakes.

# Cheese-Filled Manicotti

*To give this filling a Florentine accent, add 1/2 cup chopped cooked spinach.*

**2 cups ricotta cheese**
**1/4 cup grated Parmesan cheese**
**1 egg**
**1 cup shredded mozzarella cheese**
**3 tablespoons chopped fresh parsley**
**1 tablespoon chopped fresh basil**
**Salt and pepper to taste**

**Manicotti Pancakes, opposite**
**Italian Tomato Sauce, page 112**
**Additional Parmesan cheese**

In a medium bowl, stir together all ingredients except Manicotti Pancakes, Italian Tomato Sauce and additional Parmesan cheese, until well combined.

Spoon about 1/4 cup filling down center of pancake. Roll and place seam-side down in a shallow baking dish. Spoon Italian Tomato Sauce down the center of filled pancakes. Sprinkle with additional Parmesan cheese. Bake in a 350F (175C) oven about 20 minutes. Makes 28 to 30 pancakes.

## Variation

Omit Italian Tomato Sauce and top with Spinach-Nutmeg Sauce, page 75.

# *Mandarin Pancakes*

*With a little practice, you'll find these very simple to make.*

**1-1/2 to 1-3/4 cups all-purpose flour**
**1/4 teaspoon salt**
**3/4 cup boiling water**
**1 to 2 tablespoons sesame oil**

In a large bowl, stir together flour and salt. Make a well in center of flour, pour boiling water and about 1/2 teaspoon sesame oil in all at once. Stir quickly, making a soft dough. On a lightly floured board, knead dough 5 to 7 minutes until smooth and elastic. Cover dough and let it rest about 15 minutes.

Flour hands; shape dough into a rope about 1 inch in diameter. Cut into 16 lengths. Roll each piece into a ball and pat into a circle. Brush sesame-seed oil on tops of 8 circles. Place a plain circle on top of each oiled one. Using a rolling pin, roll each pair into a 6- to 7-inch circle. Cover while rolling remaining pancakes.

Heat a small ungreased skillet; cook each pancake pair 1 to 2 minutes on each side until lightly speckled. Remove from pan; separate pancakes. Cover to keep warm.

Pancakes may be made ahead and wrapped in foil and reheated in a 350F (175C) oven about 10 minutes. Serve with Barbecued-Meat Filling or Broiled Garlic Shrimp, opposite, or plum sauce. Makes 16 pancakes.

## Variations

*Onion-Ginger Pancakes:* Add 3 tablespoons minced green onions, including tops, and 1 tablespoon grated fresh ginger to flour.

# Barbecued-Meat Filling

*A spicy sauce adds moisture to shredded cooked meat.*

**1 tablespoon oil**
**1/2 medium onion, chopped**
**1 tablespoon dry mustard**
**1/4 cup firmly packed brown sugar**
**2 tablespoons vinegar**
**1/2 cup tomato catsup**
**1/2 cup water**
**2 cups roast beef or pork**

**Green onions, cut in 2-inch lengths**

In a medium skillet, heat oil. Add onion and sauté until softened. Stir in mustard, brown sugar, vinegar, catsup and water. Bring to a boil, reduce heat and cover. Simmer about 10 minutes. Using 2 forks, shred roasted meat and add to sauce. If desired, serve with Mandarin Pancakes, opposite, and garnish with green onions. Makes about 4-1/2 cups.

# Broiled Garlic Shrimp

**12 to 15 raw shrimp**
**2 garlic cloves, crushed**
**1/4 cup melted butter**
**1/4 teaspoon Chinese five-spice powder**

Preheat broiler. Shell shrimp and remove veins. In a small bowl, combine garlic, butter and five-spice powder. Dip shrimp into butter mixture; thread on a skewer and place on a broiler rack.

Broil shrimp 4 to 5 minutes, turn over and baste with butter mixture. Serve at once. Makes 4 to 5 servings.

# *Potato Latkes*

*In Jewish homes, these pancakes are called* latkes.
*I always think of them as the perfect dish to be served
with sauerbraten and a generous helping of
applesauce.*

**4 raw potatoes, peeled**
**1 small onion, grated**
**1/4 cup fine cracker crumbs, matzoh meal or
  all-purpose flour**
**1 tablespoon chopped fresh parsley, if desired**
**Salt and pepper to taste**

**Oil for frying**

Grate potatoes and place in a colander; press or squeeze
out as much liquid as possible. In a medium bowl,
combine all ingredients. If potatoes still contain a large
amount of liquid, increase cracker crumbs, matzoh meal,
or all-purpose flour to make mixture hold together.

In a large heavy skillet, heat 1 to 2 tablespoons oil.
Carefully spoon about 2 tablespoons mixture into oil.
Press lightly to form fritter. When edges begin to brown,
turn and lightly press again and cook other side. Place
on absorbent paper or paper towel. Cover and keep
warm. If necessary, add more oil to skillet and continue
cooking pancakes. Serve with Apple Chutney, opposite,
or sour cream. Makes 12 pancakes.

# *Apple Chutney*

*Of course applesauce is always good with latkes, but this chutney adds a refreshing tartness to the classic combination.*

**2 lbs. apples, peeled, chopped**
**1 small onion, chopped**
**3 tablespoons dried currants or dried cherries**
**1 cup cider vinegar**
**1/3 cup firmly packed brown sugar**
**1/2 teaspoon ground ginger**
**Dash nutmeg**
**Dash ground cloves**

In a large saucepan, simmer apples, onion, currants or cherries and vinegar until apples are very soft. Add sugar, ginger, nutmeg and cloves; stir until sugar is completely dissolved. Continue cooking about 10 minutes. If you like a chunky sauce, serve now. For a smoother sauce, place mixture, half at a time, in a food processor or blender. Process to desired consistency. Makes 4 to 6 servings.

# Macaroni Frittata

*Expect compliments when presenting this colorful combination. Sometimes called an* omelet—*other times a* pancake—*it's an ideal way to serve vegetables with or without pasta.*

**4 eggs**
**1 tablespoon cornstarch**
**1 tablespoon capers**
**6 or 7 black olives, sliced**
**1 tablespoon chopped fresh parsley**
**1 tablespoon olive oil**
**2 tablespoons butter**
**1/4 medium onion, chopped**
**1 red bell pepper, chopped (1/2 cup)**
**1 cup cooked macaroni**
**Salt and pepper to taste**

In a medium bowl, beat eggs and cornstarch. Stir in capers, olives and parsley; set aside.

In a 9-inch ovenproof skillet, heat oil and butter over medium heat. Add onion and red pepper; sauté until softened. Add macaroni and salt and pepper to taste; stir together until heated. Remove from heat. Pour egg mixture over all. Reduce heat to low, cover and cook 5 to 7 minutes.

Place skillet under a broiler and cook about 5 minutes or until top is set and firm. Loosen edges and cut into wedges. Serve with Creamy Spinach & Walnut Pesto, opposite, or Tuna Sauce, page 65, or sliced fresh tomatoes. Makes 6 servings.

# *Creamy Spinach & Walnut Pesto*

*Try this quick uncooked sauce when time is short. For a more pronounced nut flavor, use toasted nuts.*

**1 cup packed, fresh spinach leaves**
**2 garlic cloves or garlic salt to taste**
**1/2 cup chopped walnuts**
**2 tablespoons olive oil**
**1/4 cup Parmesan cheese**
**1/4 cup plain yogurt**
**2 tablespoons cream cheese**
**3 tablespoons lemon juice**
**1/4 teaspoon ground nutmeg**
**1 tablespoon chopped fresh chives or**
 **1 green onion top**
**Salt and pepper to taste**

Combine all ingredients in a blender or food processor, process until well blended. It will be necessary to stop the machine a few times and scrape down mixture from the sides. Cover and refrigerate until needed; bring to room temperature before using. Makes 1-1/2 cups.

# *Drop Scones*

*These are also known as* Scottish pancakes. *In Scotland you'd serve them at teatime with butter and jam.*

**1-1/2 cups all-purpose flour**
**1 teaspoon cream of tartar**
**1/2 teaspoon baking soda**
**2 tablespoons sugar**
**Pinch of salt**
**1 tablespoon maple syrup, corn syrup or molasses**
**1 egg**
**3/4 cup milk**

Preheat a nonstick griddle or lightly oiled heavy skillet. In a medium bowl, blender or food processor, mix all ingredients.

Using preheated griddle or skillet, pour or spoon about 1/8 cup batter for each scone. Cook scones until bubbles appear and edges look slightly dry. Turn over and continue cooking until lightly browned. Place cooked scones on one half of a clean cloth and fold other half over to keep them warm and moist. Serve warm or cold with Apricot-Almond Butter, opposite, or butter and raspberry or strawberry jam. Makes 16 to 20 scones.

# *Apricot-Almond Butter*

*Flavored butters are so versatile. They add a new dimension to simple pancakes and even muffins.*

**3/4 cup butter or margarine, softened**
**1/2 cup apricot preserves**
**2 teaspoons honey**
**1/4 cup toasted chopped almonds**
**1/4 teaspoon almond extract**

In a small bowl, beat butter or margarine. Add apricot preserves and continue beating until well blended. Slowly add honey, almonds and almond extract; beat until mixture is blended. Spoon into a serving bowl. Cover with foil or plastic wrap and refrigerate until needed. This can be stored up to 2 weeks. Makes about 1-1/2 cups.

# Highland Pancakes

*The cold climate in Scotland is ideal for raising oats. The Scots have used this wholesome grain in many wonderful ways.*

**1 cup quick-cooking oats**
**1 cup buttermilk**
**1 egg**
**1/2 cup water**
**1 cup all-purpose flour**
**2 tablespoons sugar**
**1 teaspoon baking soda**
**1 teaspoon baking powder**
**2 tablespoons maple syrup**
**3 tablespoons oil**

Put oats in a large mixing bowl, pour buttermilk over and let stand 15 minutes. Beat in egg and water then remaining ingredients until blended. Preheat a nonstick griddle or lightly oiled heavy skillet.

Using preheated griddle or skillet, pour or spoon about 1/4 cup batter for each pancake. Cook pancakes until bubbles appear and edges look slightly dry. Turn over and continue cooking until lightly browned. Serve with Maple Sauce, opposite, or Spicy Butter, page 115. Makes 12 to 14 pancakes.

# *Maple Sauce*

*Here is a slightly enriched maple sauce. Try adding chopped nuts or currants.*

**1 cup maple syrup**
**1 cup firmly packed brown sugar**
**1 cup half and half or diluted evaporated milk**
**2 tablespoons butter or margarine**
**1 teaspoon vanilla extract**

In a medium saucepan, combine syrup and sugar. Cook over medium heat until sugar is dissolved. Bring to a boil. Stirring constantly, cook about 2 minutes. Remove from heat; stir in half and half or evaporated milk, butter or margarine and vanilla. Makes about 2-1/2 cups.

**Tip:** For a more festive presentation, top pancakes with plain or vanilla-flavored yogurt, Maple Sauce and sliced fresh strawberries.

# *Dessert Crêpes*

*The French call these delicate pancakes,* crêpes; *in Hungary they're called* palacsinta; *Germany knows them as* palatschinken. *Generally they're served as dessert, but they can also be wrapped around nonsweet or savory fillings.*

**3 eggs**
**1 cup milk**
**1 tablespoon sugar**
**1/2 cup club soda**
**1/2 cup orange juice**
**1-1/4 cups all-purpose flour**
**1 teaspoon vanilla extract**
**1 tablespoon melted butter or oil**

### Oil for frying

Combine all ingredients in a medium bowl, blender or food processor; mix until blended. Let batter rest about 30 minutes. Batter will be thin.

Lightly brush a crêpe pan or 6- to 7-inch skillet with oil. Pour about 2 tablespoons batter into pan, immediately tilt pan so batter covers the bottom. Cook until surface looks dry and edges are lacy and brown. Turn and brown other side, this takes about 5 seconds; do not burn. Remove from pan and stack with waxed paper between crêpes. Repeat until all batter is used. Fill as desired. Makes 18 to 20 crêpes.

### Variation

Omit club soda and orange juice and substitute equal amount of regular milk. Use remaining ingredients listed in recipe.

# Dessert-Crêpe Fillings

*This delicate pancake can also be filled with ice cream, jam or fresh fruit.*

*Apricot-Walnut Filling:* In a small bowl, combine 1 (16-ounce) can drained chopped apricots with 1/3 cup chopped walnuts and 1 tablespoon brandy. For each crêpe, spread about 1 tablespoon filling in center. Roll or fold as desired. Sprinkle top with finely chopped walnuts. Makes about 2 cups.

*Apple-Raisin Filling:* In a small bowl, combine 1-1/2 cups cooked sliced apples, 1/4 cup raisins, 1/4 teaspoon ground cinnamon and 1/2 teaspoon vanilla extract. For each crêpe, spread about 1 tablespoon filling in center. Roll or fold as desired. Makes about 1-3/4 cups.

*Mixed-Nut Filling:* In a small bowl, combine 1/4 cup each toasted chopped almonds, walnuts and hazelnuts. Stir in 1/4 cup sugar, 1/4 teaspoon ground cinnamon and 1 teaspoon unsweetened cocoa powder. For each crêpe, sprinkle about 1 tablespoon nut mixture in center. Roll or fold as desired. Drizzle chocolate sauce on top and sprinkle with additional nuts. Makes about 1 cup.

*Whipped Cream & Fruit Filling:* Whip 1 cup whipping cream with 2 teaspoons powdered sugar until it mounds nicely. Mash 1/2 cup fresh or thawed frozen berries, such as raspberries, blueberries or blackberries. Fold into whipped cream. For each crêpe, spread 1 tablespoon filling over half of crêpe; fold over and garnish with remaining whipped cream and berries. Makes about 2-1/2 cups.

# MORE RELISHES & TOPPINGS

Many times I like to vary the toppings, sort of mix and match according to how the mood strikes me. I've included some additional topping and relish recipes to help you begin your own experimenting.

There are times when a simple flavored butter seems fitting as the only topping necessary. I make three flavors at a time and refrigerate them in attractive serving bowls with lids. If you don't have tops, cover them with plastic wrap or foil. These little bowls of flavor also make a nice gift. Accenting and contrasting flavors can bring about unexpected rewards. Don't be timid, try different combinations.

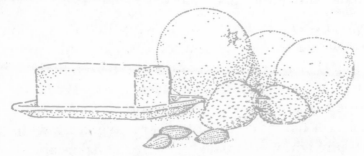

# Recipes

Italian Tomato Sauce

White Sauce

Plum Relish

Orange-Honey Butter

Maple-Pecan Butter

Jamberry Butter

Spicy Butter

Cold Chili Sauce

Cold Beet Relish

# Italian Tomato Sauce

*Here are two easy sauces.*

**3 tablespoons olive oil**
**1 cup chopped onion**
**2 garlic cloves, minced**
**1 (8-oz.) can tomato sauce**
**2 fresh tomatoes, chopped**
**1 tablespoon sugar**
**2 tablespoons chopped fresh parsley**
**2 teaspoons dried-leaf basil**
**1 teaspoon dried-leaf oregano**
**Salt and pepper to taste**

In a medium saucepan, heat oil over medium heat. Add onion and garlic; sauté until softened. Add remaining ingredients and bring to a boil. Reduce heat and simmer 10 to 15 minutes. Makes about 2 cups.

# White Sauce

**1/4 cup butter**
**1/4 cup all-purpose flour**
**1 cup milk or chicken broth**
**2/3 cup half and half or milk**
**Dash dried-leaf thyme**
**Salt and pepper to taste**

In a small saucepan, melt butter over medium heat and stir in flour. Slowly stir in milk or broth; cook, stirring constantly until sauce is thickened and smooth. Stir in half and half or milk and thyme. Season with salt and pepper to taste. Makes about 2 cups.

# *Plum Relish*

*A wonderful combination of flavors that can be made ahead, and is great with broiled meats or poultry.*

**1 (16-oz.) can purple plums with juice**
**1/2 medium onion, chopped**
**1/4 cup chopped dates**
**1 cup raspberry vinegar or cider vinegar**
**3/4 cup sugar**
**1 apple, chopped**
**1/4 teaspoon ground allspice**
**1/4 teaspoon ground ginger**

Cut plums in half and remove pits. In a medium saucepan, combine all ingredients including juice from plums. Cook, stirring occasionally, over medium heat until onion and apple are tender and juice is thickened.

Remove from heat and cool slightly. Spoon plum mixture into jars or a container with a tight-fitting lid. Cool before storing in refrigerator until needed. This can be refrigerated for two weeks. Makes about 3 cups.

## Variation

For more exotic flavors, omit plums and use canned apricots, figs, mangoes or gooseberries.

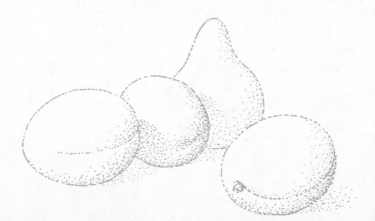

# Orange-Honey Butter

*I like to keep two or three flavored butters on hand at all times. They add interest to plain or fancy pancakes.*

**1/2 cup butter or margarine, softened**
**1/2 cup mild-flavored honey**
**2 tablespoons orange juice**
**1 tablespoon grated orange peel**

In a small bowl, beat butter or margarine. Continue beating and slowly add honey until well blended. Stir in orange juice and orange peel. Spoon into a serving bowl. Cover with foil or plastic wrap and refrigerate until needed. This can be stored up to 2 weeks. Makes about 1 cup.

# Maple-Pecan Butter

**1 cup butter or margarine, softened**
**1/4 cup firmly packed brown sugar**
**3/4 cup maple syrup**
**1/2 cup toasted chopped pecans**
**Dash ground nutmeg**

In a small bowl, beat butter or margarine. Add brown sugar and continue beating until well blended. Slowly add maple syrup; stir until mixture is blended. Stir in pecans and nutmeg. Spoon into a serving bowl. Cover with foil or plastic wrap and refrigerate until needed. This can be stored up to 2 weeks. Makes about 2 cups.

# *Jamberry Butter*

**3/4 cup butter or margarine, softened**
**1/2 cup strawberry, blueberry or other jam**
**1 tablespoon kirsch liqueur**
**1 tablespoon orange juice**

In a small bowl, beat butter or margarine. Add jam of choice and continue beating until well blended. Slowly add kirsch and orange juice; beat until mixture is blended. Spoon into a serving bowl. Cover with foil or plastic wrap and refrigerate until needed. This can be stored up to 2 weeks. Makes about 1 cup.

# *Spicy Butter*

**1/2 cup butter or margarine, softened**
**1/4 cup sugar**
**1 tablespoon corn syrup**
**1/4 teaspoon ground cinnamon**
**1/4 teaspoon ground allspice**
**1/8 teaspoon ground nutmeg**
**1/8 teaspoon ground mace**

In a small bowl, beat butter or margarine. Add sugar and continue beating until well blended. Slowly add corn syrup; beat until mixture is blended. Stir in cinnamon, allspice, nutmeg and mace until well blended. Spoon into a serving bowl. Cover with foil or plastic wrap and refrigerate until needed. This can be stored up to 2 weeks. Makes about 3/4 cup.

# Cold Chili Sauce

*Fresh herbs add extra flavor to a stir-and-serve sauce.*

**1 cup dairy sour cream**
**2 tablespoons mayonnaise**
**1/4 cup prepared chili sauce**
**1 green onion, chopped**
**1 tablespoon chopped fresh cilantro**
**2 teaspoons chopped fresh parsley**

In a small bowl, combine sour cream, mayonnaise and chili sauce. Stir in green onion, cilantro and parsley. Cover and refrigerate until needed. This can be refrigerated several days. Makes about 1-1/2 cups.

# Cold Beet Relish

*A beautiful pink dish highlighted with chives and walnuts—truly as pretty as a picture!*

**1 (16-oz.) can or jar sliced pickled beets**
**1/2 cup dairy sour cream or plain yogurt**
**1/4 cup chopped walnuts**
**1 tablespoon chopped fresh chives or cilantro**

Drain beets and place in a serving bowl. Gently stir in sour cream. Sprinkle with nuts and chives or cilantro. Cover and refrigerate until needed. Makes about 2 cups.

# *Index*